Praise for Melissa Ma

D0069392

"I have known Melissa Maimc
and I feel privileged at any opportunity to hear her speak
or teach. Melissa is delightfully funny, winsome, and a
biblically sound communicator. She is the rare speaker
who can educate while entertaining. Melissa has allowed
her struggles to plow the terrain of her own heart, making
it soft enough to bring genuine comfort to the hearts of
those fortunate enough to hear her. She unites women
with laughter, shares the right amount of herself, and
hangs around long enough to wipe away the tears. She's
the real deal."

—Nicole Johnson
Best-selling author of Fresh Brewed Life
Dramatist and Women of Faith *speaker*

"Melissa knows God intimately and shares His powerful
truth in a vulnerable, God-centered way. She leads
women to respond courageously as she models the life of
a true disciple in her messages. She is an authentic,
dependent, and disciplined disciple. Plainly, I trust her to
bring the Word to the ladies I lead."

—Megan Marshman
Director of Women's Ministries
Hume Lake Christian Camps

"Melissa has an incredible gift of connecting with her
audience in a way that is truly meaningful and authentic."

—Pastor Eric Johns
Monte Vista Chapel
Turlock, CA

Gathering Dandelions

Meditations and Musings on Faith, Fracture,
and Beauty Mistaken for a Weed

Melissa Maimone

MERULA
PRESS

Published by Merula Press.
Printed in the United States of America.

ISBN 0-692-80039-5

For Danny
You've believed in me from the beginning.

Table of Contents

Introduction *1*

1. Between Seasons 9

2. Are You Watching? 15

3. Canvas...23

4. Croaking in the Darkness..........................31

5. Crimes of Joy 37

6. Thirsty 41

7. To Protect and Serve 47

8. Naked Prayer 55

9. The Sheep of His Pasture..........................63

10. Minor Scrapes 73

11. Choice by Choice...................................79

12. Rushing Rivers......................................87

13. Inspired 93

14. The Value of a Widget..............................99

15. The Sparrow Flies Free 107

16. Diagnosis: Undefined............................111

17. Postcards & Precipices..........................119

18. Hope, of All Things 127

19. Alone ... but Not Really.........................135

20. An Unexpected Autumn 143

21. Deeper, Richer, Truer............................147

22. The Darkness and the Dawn 153

23. Getting the Hang of New Things............157

24. When the Old Bullies the New 165

25. God Creates...171

26. In the Zone..177

27. The Edges of Irises................................187

28. Remembering to Float...........................193

29. I Am..201

30. Letting Go of Feeling Bad 205

31. On Robin Williams and the Love of God ..211

32. Gathering Dandelions............................221

33. ~~Jumping~~ Falling from Trees 229

34. Surrounded 237

35. The Things I Never Got............................243

36. The KNOW-Know 251

37. Staring Down Fear 257

38. Resolution 261

39. Destined for Greatness 267

40. Is This It? 273

Acknowledgments *281*

Notes *287*

Introduction

I've always believed in God. There was never a time I doubted His existence or His power. But what I believe *about* God has changed significantly over time.

Years ago, I was positive that I was an utter disappointment to Him. I believed He wanted me, but a tidier version of me. I wanted that too. I didn't understand my tangled thoughts and feelings; they were burdensome and often brought me to dark places of depression.

Because I loathed the dark places in my mind and heart, I felt certain He did too. To present Him with the fractured chaos inside my soul would be too shameful. Too scary. Too vulnerable.

I knew that if I took the chance to turn my messy, embarrassing, confusing life over to God and He rejected me—I would truly be without hope. So I kept Him at arm's length, believing He was doing the same with me.

It took a while before my arm got really, really tired. Because of a combination of exhaustion, circumstances, and the desperate longing inside my soul, I reached out to Jesus Christ. I groped around in the dark, unsure where to look, unsure what to expect, but open to the possibility that perhaps, just maybe, He would be gracious enough to put up with me.

I could tell you the details of when Jesus became real to me, but the only part that really matters is that for the first time in my life, I became truly vulnerable before God. I brought my whole, messy, embarrassing self before His throne and waited around long enough to see what would happen. And in the midst of all those feelings and all that longing, Jesus found me. He grabbed my hand, my heart, and my soul, and He hasn't let go since.

Jesus has always upended people's preconceived notions of what they imagined Him to be, and I was no exception.

I discovered that His thoughts about almost anything, including His ideas about me, are vastly different from my own perspectives. By reading Scripture, through prayer, and with the help of friends who patiently answered my constant questions, I learned about the true Jesus.

He is the One who whispers words of love, comfort, and acceptance. He is the One who invites the weary and heavy-laden to come to Him and rest. He is the One who invites us to green pastures and still waters. He is the One who desires authenticity, no matter how messy, over pretense.

He is comfortable with the uncomfortable, and in His presence, there is no shame.

My faith has never developed in a straight line. Not even a squiggly line. It's been more like a labyrinth: gradual lefts and sharp rights, repeated steps, new routes, and just when I am sure I am getting closer to the center, I find myself headed in the opposite direction. There are paths I have retraced over and over again, yet they are never entirely the same, because Jesus always has something new for His children, even in the oldest of patterns.

Still, I assumed that at some point He would remove the parts of my being that I struggle with the most. They are of no use to me. I considered them weeds—unlovely and unpresentable. Yet in His gentle, firm way, Jesus is still upending my preconceived notions of Him.

I am discovering that my ongoing weaknesses produce a continual need of Him. Because I am unable to make sense of various aspects in my own story, I must rely on the Author to write the chapters. And because I have found nowhere else to go with my heart, I am compelled again and again to offer it back to the only One who truly understands it. In this way, I've found that the parts of me I believed He should have plucked out actually needed to be gathered and held in His arms.

This grace of God has forever changed me. I no longer hide my untidiness from Him. My prayers are at times meandering and muddled, but they are sincere. I refuse to revert back to a place of isolation, hoarding my deepest needs out of fear and faithlessness. I bring it all to Him. Embarrassment. Anxiety. Excitement. Fragility. Strength. Questions. Worship. Gratitude. Neurosis. All of it. At His feet the weeds of my life have found a place to grow and blossom into something beautiful. My joy is deep and abiding, and circumstances can't change what He has so generously planted in my soul.

If there is one lesson, one thought, one idea my heart wants you to take away from this book, it's that you have a God who always wants you to come to Him—no matter what, with everything you have or don't have.

Maybe you've believed that your experiences, your quirks, your interests, your thoughts, your worries, your deepest struggles are too trivial, too messy, or too embarrassing for Him. It's not true. He is proud of how He created you, and He is madly, deeply, and immeasurably pleased with you. Don't let anything stand in the way of getting to know the One who has perfectly formed your heart and has plans for you that are better, kinder, and more amazing than anything you ever thought possible.

Our God is constantly gathering dandelions: finding fractured people mistaken for weeds and creating bouquets of richness and beauty.

This book is a result of my being gathered up by the

love and grace of God. I pray it is an invitation and inspiration for you to live more carefree before Him, to trust His goodness, and to find the beauty in your life that you or others might have mistaken for weeds.

In Him,

Melissa

1.

Between Seasons

"There is a time for everything, and a season for every activity under the heavens."
—Ecclesiastes 3:1

I woke up this morning to the sound (and wonderful smell!) of rain. I wore my best cozy sweater and boots and bounded out the door. By 10:00 a.m., there wasn't a cloud in the sky, and the sun was out and shining brightly. I felt sweaty and itchy and walked a lot slower. In the afternoon, clouds rolled in, and a light mist began falling. Summer and fall seem to be arm-wrestling.

It happens four times a year—a change of season. Yet there are a few weeks in between those season changes when everything seems mixed up. The season we are used to is slowly giving way to the season arriving. And whether or not we jump in with both feet to the upcoming season or hang on to the last bits of the current one, these two or three weeks "between seasons" can leave us feeling overdressed and unprepared.

Sometimes we find ourselves holding on to what has been—warm days, watermelons, flip flops, and sparklers. Summer happened. It was real, it was wonderful, and there are portions of the day that will remind us summer is still around. The afternoon sun, the beach chairs leaning against the side of the house, the shell collection on the mantle, and the sunscreen still rolling around in the backseat of the car all speak of something that was warm, consistent, and good.

But now, as cooler days make intermittent appearances, you might find your boots lying right next to your sandals and your closet housing both sundresses and sweaters. Remnants of what has been mix with signs of what will be.

There are parts of life that feel the same way. There can be some wonderful, incredible, life-changing seasons that are now waning. We hold onto them because they have been good and have grown us and taught us much about God, ourselves, and others. Those times might have included tears, hard lessons, and deep wounds, too, yet even those have served a purpose. We can be deeply grateful for all of the happiness and heartbreak that beautiful season offered.

But there are desires you have, dreams to pursue, and doors to open that are waiting for you. Signs of a new season are always emerging. What has been known and cherished is making room for what is new and unexplored. This can be overwhelming at times, leaving you feeling unprepared and improperly dressed. Ecclesiastes 3:1 says, *"There is a time for everything, and a season for every activity under the heavens"*—which means that even if grief and hope intertwine in your heart and you don't know whether to laugh or cry, this season of change has been ordained by God.

I'm learning that the change of season is as important as the season itself. That small, unique window of time is when we can experience what has been and what will be at the very same time. It's altogether confusing, exhilarating, and more than a bit scary.

Maybe this is your time "between seasons." For the moment, I hope you embrace it, even if we both end up wearing fuzzy socks with summer sandals.

- Are there areas of your life that are moving from one season to another?

- In reflecting on seasons that are waning, what lessons have you learned about God, yourself, and those around you?

- In looking forward to the upcoming seasons in your life, what do you anticipate with joy? What do you fear? What do you need from God in this time of change?

Dear Abba, You are the source of the seasons. You created this earth with a sun that rises and sets, tides that roll in and out, and winds that bring both warmth and chill. Help me to embrace the changes I experience. Allow me to learn and grow from them. May I offer assurance and empathy to those experiencing their own changes. And in all the seasons of my life, may I be faithful, knowing that every season (and the ones in between) is ordained, planned, and cared for by You, my steadfast Father. Amen.

2.

Are You Watching?

"Are not two sparrows sold for a penny?
Yet not one of them will fall to the ground outside
your Father's care. And even the very hairs
of your head are all numbered."
—Matthew 10:29–30

"Watch me, Mom! Are you watching? Here I go!"

I looked up from the magazine I'd been trying to read to watch my son, Cole, jump into the pool in the exact same way he had done seven times before. A few seconds later, his head popped up out of the water like a cork.

"Did you see me, Mom? Did you see my jump? It was my best one!"

"Yes! It was fantastic!"

I lifted my magazine once more, ready to go beyond the opening paragraph I'd now read seven times in the past 10 minutes.

"I'm going to go even higher this time. Watch me!"

Down went the magazine.

Splash went Cole.

"Did you see me?"

"Yes, it was wonderful!"

And so it continued.

Summer days at the pool were not always as relaxing as I'd hoped. My fantasies of lying luxuriously on a chaise lounge with a magazine, sipping on a cold glass of lemon-flavored water were replaced with the reality of slathering sunscreen onto squirming kids, yelling at those same kids to slow down and walk-not-run, getting the last sip from a leftover (warm) juice box, and never finishing a magazine article. And of course, my summers were filled with those three words, "Are you watching?"

Observing the kids jump into the pool in a variety of poses was fun for a few moments. But it was clear they wanted my undivided attention the entire time, which quickly became wearisome.

Interestingly, "Are You watching?" is a question we ask of God, too. When life is confusing, painful, or overwhelming, maybe you wonder if He's reading a magazine. Or maybe you imagine He is wearied by the same feelings, the same worries, and the same fears that repeat themselves in your life. The issues that weigh on our hearts can be perpetually and frustratingly similar, no matter how the particulars of our circumstances vary.

What I believe Cole really wanted to know, and what our hearts cry out to know from God, is the deeper question: "Are you SEEING me?" Truthfully, we don't want to know if God is just watching; we need to know He is seeing. We are desperate to know that He's not glancing up between sentences from a magazine, not placating us with hollow exclamations, but really, truly, seeing into the deepest core of who we are and what we need.

I hope you are blessed by at least a few people who can see you—all your strengths, weaknesses, victories, and defeats. These people are witnesses to your life. They are acolytes pointing you in the right direction, affirming and encouraging your heart. We are designed to need people, so their presence fulfills very real, God-designed needs. But people, by very nature of our humanness, will never see all of the parts of our soul that require unwavering attention.

It is God alone, the One who counts the hairs on your head and formed your yet-to-be-born body, who can see you for all you are, all you need, and all you are meant to be.

God isn't just watching you. He sees you. He sees your predicaments, your heartbreaks, your quirks, and how reruns of *Little House on the Prairie* still make you cry. He is with you when you succeed at new things or fail once again at the same old things.

Even so, it's one thing for us to understand this truth in our head, and it's another thing entirely to experience being seen.

To experience being seen, we must slow down. We need to breathe in, breathe out, and look around with intention. When we look for God in every moment, we will find God looking at us. We must endeavor to live a vulnerable life, one that declares to Him our need to be seen. We can—no, we must—ask Abba over and over again, "Are You watching?" not because we seek to get His attention (He's never not paying attention) but because every time we ask, we declare our utter dependence on Him.

And every time we ask, He will answer in the affirmative. Every single time. And we can jump into the deep waters of His undying attention, pop up like a cork, and know we are seen by the One who loves us most.

- How do you long to be seen and known?

- Have you withheld from God your need to be seen because it feels too vulnerable?

- Do you believe that God doesn't just watch you, but rather He sees you—all you are and all He created you to be? Let your honest answer become a cry of your heart or a song of praise to the One who is not merely watching, but seeing you in this moment.

Dear Abba, my frail heart needs to know You are intimately familiar with all of my being: heart, soul, and mind. I need to know You are not just watching me but that You are seeing me. I need to know there is not one thought, one action, one fear, one joy that misses Your attention. I need to know that I am not alone in traversing this life and that You are vigilant in the complexities of my circumstances. I confess, sometimes I wonder if You are reading a magazine. I'm sorry I doubt. I ask You, my all-knowing, all-loving God, to show me again that You see me, know me, and love me. Help me to breathe in, breathe out, and intentionally look for You in every moment. In doing so, I trust that You will, over and over again, reveal Your attentiveness, Your faithfulness, and Your unwavering love in the places You know I need that most.

Amen.

3.

Canvas

*"For now we see only a reflection as in a mirror;
then we shall see face to face. Now I know in part;
then I shall know fully, even as I am fully known."*
—1 Corinthians 13:12

You are an unfinished work of art, a painting still on the easel with bright splashes of pigment and spots of blank canvas. Perhaps your life is fragmented, boxed in and angular like a Picasso. Or your future looks hazy and slightly out of focus like a Monet. Or maybe your thoughts, like mine, are more like a Jackson Pollock—messy, scattered, and seemingly random. Whether you are a Rembrandt or a Rothko, the full masterpiece of your life is still in progress. Great art takes time, you know. A true artist won't be rushed, and you are in the hands of the Master Artist. I was reminded of this recently by my cousin-in-law, Lee.

Lee is a fantastic artist; she paints, she draws, she writes, she makes jewelry, and she builds her own furniture. I adore her. She is free, funny, and definitely the artistic type. She lives in a cute one-bedroom apartment filled with paintbrushes, canvases, random pieces of wood, and interesting books. Her paintings cover almost every square inch of the walls. Her work is modern and beautiful, and her canvases are thick with the layers of the paint she uses. When I visit her, it takes every bit of self-control for me not to reach out and touch the rough edges and smooth strokes of the thick paint on her artwork.

Recently I asked Lee if she would paint something for my home. I gave her the canvas and armed her with a variety of pictures and paintings that inspire me as well as a CD of music that moves me. I told her to paint whatever comes to her imagination.

It's been almost three months since I commissioned her. She told me that the reason why it takes so long to complete a painting like hers is that she must wait a week between each layer of paint before she can resume her work. Lee likes a lot of layers.

So does God.

God wants His people to have depth and substance and lives that reflect beautiful light and bright colors. He desires for His beloved to have places of the deep darkness of struggle and pain, too, because those things create unparalleled beauty that is reflective of the Artist Himself. The people who allow Him to work and live in the deepest areas of their hearts as well as the brightest parts of their souls are rich in wisdom and compassion, and He wants that for each of us.

The Lord likes His works of art to have depth, texture, and areas of transparency where the canvas of the story shows through. He has mixed a pigment into your soul that is unique to you, and He delights in the subtle differences of color created by His hand. He knows every brushstroke and layer on your canvas—your history, how you've been formed and influenced and even wounded in the process of His work.

He likes layers.

But as Lee pointed out, layers take time. They do not come easily, and they require enormous amounts of patience. Layers require the humility and vulnerability of remaining unfinished for long periods of time.

Layers mean that not everything is seen on the surface. Each of us has aspects of our heart that remain hidden under the surface, not known by anyone else, but intimately understood by the Creator who lovingly placed them there. They are meant for His eyes only. But those things underneath mean that the colors covering them will leap off the canvas and inspire people to explore their own layers and beauty.

Vincent van Gogh said, *"I long so much to make beautiful things. But beautiful things require effort—and disappointment and perseverance."*[1] Van Gogh understood the pain of being unfinished. He knew the time it takes to add layers and depth in order to create something spectacular.

You are an unfinished work. The canvas is still wet, and there are more layers to be added. Just as Van Gogh observed, you will experience tremendous pain, disappointment, and strained perseverance along the way.

But you are in the hands of the Master. And He is always doing something amazing.

One day, in the not-too-distant future, the Master will finish His work in you. You will get to see it complete, framed, and on display. He will reveal His masterpiece, and all these layers, all this time, all the unfinished parts of your life will make sense and you will be grateful for every stroke made. For now, we remain unfinished, trusting that the time it takes for each layer will produce the completeness our souls long for. And it will, because He is faithful.

- What layers reside under what most people see of you on the surface? How have these layers informed and brought depth and color to your life?

- How have effort, disappointment, and perseverance created beautiful things in you?

- What do you hope to see when God reveals His final, finished work in you?

Oh, great Artist, creator of my being and muralist of my soul, how I long to step back and see Your work complete in me! But I know You will not be finished until my last breath is taken. You are still mixing pigment and finding new shades of color to add to my story that bring complexity and beauty in every stroke of Your brush. Thank You for the painstaking detail You give to every corner of this canvas. May Your work in me be steady and patient. May each layer You add be done with care and intention, and every touch be heavy with possibility and promise. When I cannot understand what You are creating, when I do not have Your perspective, when I wonder if my life is more of a mess than a masterpiece, I ask not to see the whole picture, but instead for a deeper trust of Your artistry. I offer to You this canvas of my life and ask You to do Your work.

Amen.

4.

Croaking in the Darkness

*"In the same way, the Spirit helps us in our
weakness. We do not know what we ought to pray
for, but the Spirit himself intercedes for us
through wordless groans."*
—Romans 8:26

Most of the time, my hope is *in* Jesus. Other times?
The ones I hate to admit, yet still occur? I hope *for*
Jesus.

Most of the time I believe He is right with me—by
my side—His Holy Spirit filling me. And then there
are those "3:00-in-the-morning-and-I'm-going-to-
die" moments. (Okay, hours.)

The hours of darkness.

The times when I cannot feel His presence, remember His peace, or find His power. Some people experience it as worry or anxiety. For me, it comes roaring out of the darkness into stage four panic.

Having a panic attack, especially at 3:00 a.m., is like being woken up to getting punched in the stomach while being suffocated with a pillow.

The worst part isn't even the racing heart or the consuming paralysis. It's that all rational thinking is lost. Accusations, worries, insults, and fragmented thinking race toward me, tripping over one another in a frenzy to reach my mind and heart. In my frozen state, they find their target.

Sometimes the only word that I can muster amid all the noise is His name.

Oh, Jesus.

Jesus.

It is the prayer of the desperate ... of the humbled ... of the needy.

Panic, as with pain, worry, or grief, rarely allows for reason. It shuts out order and smothers strength. And sometimes we can only croak out a whisper in the madness, "Oh, Jesus." It's not pretty. It's not fluent. But Jesus has never been interested in wordiness. He prefers honesty to eloquence every single time.

In Scripture He tells a story about two men praying in a synagogue (Luke 18:9–14). One is a Pharisee who uses a lot of big words to express his big thoughts to a God he thinks is small enough to be impressed by his dog and pony show. The other is a tax collector who doesn't offer more than a croak to the God who deserves so much more. But it's a sincere croak. And Jesus likes that sincerity and humility.

I will never get used to the occasional nighttime

visits from my friendly neighborhood panic attack. But they definitely strip away any pretense between me and God. For that, I am grateful.

And when the panic dissipates and my Savior finds me in the darkness and envelops me with His serenity beyond understanding, I am awestruck by His goodness. And once more, this time in overwhelming gratitude, I whisper into the dark the only words my trembling lips can form:

"Oh, Jesus, Jesus."

- When you are in a time of desperation, whom do you call out to?

- What are your prayers like when you need God most?

- Can you allow yourself to be desperate for God?

Dear Abba, there are times when words of prayer form on my lips without strain, words of praise and gratitude, confession and need. I like those times. But then there are those hours (or days or months) when I'm so overwhelmed that I cannot do more than groan in Your direction. Those are desperate, fearful times. When I am croaking in the darkness, I am grateful that You have given me Your Holy Spirit, translating my groans into prayers. You have equipped me for every season of this life. I am secure in Your provision. Oh, Jesus, find me in the darkness and pull me into Your light. Let the night give way to morning, that my joy is once again renewed in You. And even when it's so dark I cannot see Your face nor feel Your presence, I will trust in Your goodness and grace just the same, for You are forever faithful.

Amen.

5.

Crimes of Joy

*"In this world you will have trouble. But take heart!
I have overcome the world."*
—John 16:33b

It's been an awesome day. The pumpkin spice latte is back; I actually liked how my rear end looked in my jeans; I finally found a mascara that doesn't smear; I snagged a great parking space at Costco; and I took a blissful 45-minute nap. Oh, first-world happiness!

With all that is taking place in this world, in the lives of others, and even in my own life, it seems like a crime to get happy about mascara. There's too much to consider, remember, and worry about, right?

Give me 5 minutes to mull those things over, and I'll get decidedly introspective and morose. Give me 10 minutes and I'm ready to don a beret, light up an unfiltered cigarette, and listen to jazz music in a smoky gin joint with a bartender named Leroy.

It's not that the serious things aren't, well, serious. They are. It's just that the serious stuff can make us feel guilty about the frivolous. In truth, the more difficult a person's life, the less the peripheral things matter. Yet similar to how a blurred background in a photograph focuses our attention on the subject, the peripheral in life directs us to the focal point.

Frederick Buechner writes, *"Here is the world. Beautiful and terrible things will happen. Don't be afraid."*[1]

Laughing so hard you cry (or leak, if you're like me), singing out loud in the car, making up silly dances on the kitchen floor, and watching those cat videos on YouTube are all an affront to the forces that want us to be afraid and circumspect. Don't submit. Don't get pushed around by the voices in your head and in this world that insist there's something to fear. Circumstances that require your serious attention have no right to demand you forfeit your joy. As a matter of fact, the more serious things are in your life, the more you might need that pumpkin spice latte—and to really, really enjoy it.

Terrible things are happening. Be compassionate. Be mindful. Be faithful. Don't be afraid. And when you are, don't give up on what makes you smile and brings you joy. Embrace the beautiful. Enjoy the peripheral—even if it seems like a crime to do so. It's a beautiful and terrible world. We have nothing to fear. Laugh, watch, nap, dance, sing, and sip.

- What circumstances in your life have been demanding that you forfeit your joy?

- What "joy crime spree" can you commit today?

Dear Abba, sometimes I get so afraid of all that is happening in this world, in the lives of my friends, and even in my own life, it feels like a crime to be happy. Yet You invite me to "take heart!" In other words, You have given me full permission to go on a "joy crime spree." By Your grace, let me laugh heartily, sip deeply, and declare boldly that I will not forfeit my joy to anything. Let my actions be an affront to all that threatens to steal my joy in You. And the next time I get worn down with worry and fear of the world, remind me again that You have overcome it. Oh—and maybe remind me to enjoy a latte, too. Thanks, Abba. I love You.

Amen.

6.

Thirsty

"Come, all you who are thirsty, come to the waters."
—Isaiah 55:1

In 1931, Wall was a small, dusty town on the outskirts of the badlands of South Dakota. The population was just over 300. That same year, Ted and Dorothy Hustead opened a drugstore that offered not only prescriptions, but also a variety of over-the-counter remedies, ice cream, books, and small toys. It was a typical small-town drugstore. But for the first five years, business was not exactly booming.

Because of the local patrons, the Husteads' store hung on by a financial thread, but their dried-up business mirrored the dry heat of the town. The cars on the highway kicked up dust as people drove through Wall, but rarely to Wall.

In 1936, near to closing their doors permanently, Dorothy had an idea. She suggested they offer something free of charge to the travelers driving by. Ted liked the idea, too, so he created clever signs advertising their free offer and placed them along the highway. Soon enough, people were stopping at Wall Drug, taking Ted and Dorothy up on their free offer. And wouldn't you know it? Those same people spent money on merchandise as well.

Today, Wall Drug brings in more than $5 million in annual revenue. The town of Wall, South Dakota, is still small and dusty. But people no longer just drive through. What did Ted and Dorothy offer to people, free of charge, that changed the Husteads' dying business to a thriving must-stop shop?[1]

Water.

Yep. That's it. Water.

But to a weary traveler in the middle of nowhere, a free glass of ice-cold water is about the best thing one could offer.

Psalm 63:1 (ESV) says, *"O God, you are my God; earnestly I seek you; my soul thirsts for you; my flesh faints for you, as in a dry and weary land where there is no water."*

As this psalmist expresses, sometimes our souls feel so parched we cannot swallow properly.

Jesus said, *"Anyone who drinks the water I give will never thirst—not ever. The water I give will be an artesian spring within, gushing fountains of endless life"* (John 4:14, MSG).

Jesus Christ offers an ice-cold glass of water to our weary, thirsty souls. He invites us to come to Him, cool off, and drink deeply. Often, though, I am so busy driving through my life and my problems that I forget how much I need a cold glass of water along the way. Then His Word reminds me again that the Living Water I need is extended freely, ready for taking.

There is a sign in Amsterdam that reads, "5,397 miles to Wall Drug, Wall, S.D., USA." Similar signs exist in Vietnam, Kenya, Zaire, Paris, Rome, and across the United States. From anywhere in the world, people are invited to come to Wall Drug for a free, ice-cold glass of water. It's a pretty amazing thing! A few years ago, I had the opportunity to wander around the now city-block-size Wall Drug, sipping my free water. I loved it.

Each one of us has been invited to the free, thirst-quenching, grace-filled love of Jesus Christ. Like I did in Wall Drug, we can wander around in this grace we've been given and we can drink deeply from that which is abundant and free. On this hot and sometimes dusty journey of life, that's the best kind of news for this weary traveler.

- What does your soul thirst for in this dry and weary land?

- Are you drinking deeply of the love and grace of Jesus Christ? Why or why not?

O God, You are my God; earnestly I seek You;
my soul thirsts for You. I am a weary traveler in this
world, and at times I forget You are the Living Water
right in front of me, offering the satisfaction I so
desperately desire. Fill me again with Your Spirit,
Your peace, Your grace. No matter where I am in this
world, I pray I orient myself in Your direction. May I
live in the full confidence that You will always meet
my innermost needs. And may I drink deeply from
that which is abundant and free: my Living Water,
my soul satisfaction, Jesus Christ.
Amen.

7.

To Protect and Serve

"God is our refuge and strength,
an ever-present help in trouble."
—Psalm 46:1

I changed my outfit seven times. What to wear for an evening of patrolling the streets, keeping the peace, and securing the city until the wee hours of the morning is a dilemma. I was going on a ride-along with the Los Angeles Police Department (LAPD) and wanted to be prepared for anything.

I settled on jeans, a black top, and of course, my cowboy boots. After all, I needed to let the criminals know there was a new sheriff in town. Okay, a new "ride-alonger" in town. I've wanted to experience a ride-along with the police for as long as I can remember. So when the opportunity presented itself, I was more than ready to go.

I met my partner, Sergeant Brian, and hopped into the front seat of his patrol car. Off we went onto the mean streets of the San Fernando Valley in California. It took everything in me not to pelt him with questions: What does this button do? Where do we go first? Can I turn on the siren? When do I get a weapon? Should I wear a badge? Can we get donuts just for the irony of it? Am I allowed to Mirandize someone? (I've watched plenty of episodes of *Law & Order*. I know the speech.)

However, I contained myself and let him ask the questions. After getting to know one another a bit, he asked me, "What do you think you can handle tonight?"

"What do you mean?" I asked.

"I don't know what will happen tonight. It might be really boring. But if something happens and things get rough, I need to know if you are prepared for that or if you'd prefer to be dropped off at the station first," Sergeant Brian explained.

I had to think about that one. I knew the evening could hold anything. But could I handle what I might see? After some thought, I told him that I believed I could and that I am not entirely naive to what might occur. (At this point, I was relieved I'd kept the siren question to myself.)

Since Brian is a sergeant, we did not go out on a lot of calls. Most get handled by patrol officers. He only goes to the ones that require a supervisor by law or at the request of the officers, which meant we drove around quite a bit before getting our first call. We had a lot of time to talk. I found Sergeant Brian to be conversational and informative throughout the night.

At one point, I asked him if he had any funny or

fantastic stories to share. He hesitated, and I saw something flicker across his face; then he told me that most of his stories were probably more sad or bloody than fun. Then he went quiet. He wasn't being dramatic or unkind. Rather, I believe he was being protective.

The mission "To protect and serve" is emblazoned on every LAPD vehicle. Seeing those words makes me feel safe, like someone is standing between me and the bad guys. It feels good. These men and women are charged with bringing peace where there is strife and protection where it is needed for people they've never met, knowing they may be disrespected, criticized, or worse by the same citizens they've sworn to serve.

Sergeant Brian knew that if we came upon a scene of violence, I wasn't going to be able to "unsee" what I would witness. I imagine that in his hesitation before he answered me, he pictured people and situations that were permanently embedded in his memory.

We may hear stories on the news or online where a police officer protected or rescued someone from imminent danger. We marvel at their bravery. That is the "protecting and serving" we see.

But what have we been protected from that we will never understand? There are people who see terrible things so we don't have to. They stand in the line of fire and take on the mantle of protection so the rest of us can live undaunted by some of the complexities of this world. I am not suggesting we are living in a bubble. We have all faced agonizing aspects of life and experienced difficult events. But if we are lucky, those things are not a normal part of our lives.

How many things are we protected from in this life? Only God knows. He tried to prevent Adam and Eve from eating from the tree of the knowledge of good and evil. When they gave in to temptation, their souls could not "unsee" their nakedness, their shame.

In this life, we are all exposed to more than we should be. But I suspect we are protected from more than we know.

I assume most of us live grateful lives. We love our families and friends and hopefully don't take for granted that we live in homes with running water, insulation, and air conditioning. But there is an abundance of things we'll never know about. Blessings we've received but never recognized. Ways we've been protected that amount to a flicker on the face of a sergeant for us but countless grim memories for him.

What more has God protected us from? How has He been our help in times of trouble that we will never know about? What we are blissfully unaware of simply because something didn't happen that could have? What blessings are right in front of us that we've taken for granted because their familiarity means we don't even think about them anymore? Our God is our refuge and strength in ways we can see and in ways we know nothing about. He has vowed to protect and serve His children, and He is faithful to do so.

Sergeant Brian and I went out on a couple of (nonviolent) calls that night, and I loved every minute. I inquired if there were openings for a professional "ride-alonger," but I was politely declined. I never did get to wear a badge or Mirandize anyone, but I have the feeling that's just fine for my soul. And I am grateful.

- How can you better see the everyday blessings right in front of you?

- Who are the people in your life protecting you from that which you would not be able to "unsee"?

Oh, Father, thank You for being my ever-present help in times of trouble. You are both mighty and humble, powerful to show me Your great faithfulness, yet silently working on my behalf even when I don't see it. Thank You for the people who give their lives to protect and serve our communities and our homeland. I praise You for the security and grace You provide through them. Open my eyes to see the blessings right in front of me, that I may live a deeply grateful life. And thank You for the blessings You give that I will never know about.

Amen.

8.

Naked Prayer

"Ask and it will be given to you;
seek and you will find;
knock and the door will be opened to you."
—Matthew 7:7

"I have a question," Rachel whispered.

Her eyes glanced around to make sure we were alone. I leaned forward so I could hear her better and nodded my head for her to continue.

"Is it okay to pray in the shower?"

My confused expression told her she needed to elaborate.

"I mean," she continued, "is it okay to pray to God

in the shower, because, you know ... I'm naked in the shower. I'm not sure if it's disrespectful. But it's where I can think and so it's where I end up praying. But if it's not okay, then I won't do it anymore."

It's one of the more unusual questions I've been asked in ministry. It remains one of my favorites. Rachel looked at me in all seriousness as she asked; this was important to her.

I love that she felt the gravity of speaking to the Creator of the universe and that she wanted the time and the place of her prayers to be appropriate.

I love even more that she prayed naked.

God's original design was for Adam and Eve to be naked and unashamed in His presence. He didn't want anything to come between Him and His children. It was only after sin divided them that they found the fig leaf fashionable.

God is calling to us and coming after us—offering us

a deep, eternal connection. He doesn't want to be apart from us, but He does give choices: to love Him or not, to respond or not, to ignore Him or not. This means He allows Himself to be vulnerable to us. His invitation is that we become (and remain) vulnerable to Him.

To be naked is to be exposed. It's to allow the unkempt, less-than-perfect, private aspects of ourselves to be seen—to be unguarded, unprotected, and undignified.

The Bible is filled with "naked prayers": cries out to God that are unrehearsed and unpolished, vulnerable in their need and gratitude.

> *"My soul is in deep anguish. How long, LORD, how long?"* (Psalm 6:3)

> *"My soul glorifies the Lord and my spirit rejoices in God my Savior."* (Luke 1:46–47)

> *"God, have mercy on me, a sinner."* (Luke 18:13)

"My God, my God, why have you forsaken me?"
(Mark 15:34)

Our prayers don't need to be fancy; they need to be honest. Our prayers don't require dignity; they require sincerity. They can be said on the freeway or on our knees.

With a bowed head or dancing feet.

At our best moments and on our worst days.

Shouted or whispered.

Prayers to God can be spoken while wearing our pajamas, our Sunday best, and even our birthday suits.

I shared some of these thoughts with Rachel. "Oh, good!" she said, clearly relieved. "I always feel closer to God when I pray in the shower."

Whatever the attire or place, hopefully all of our prayers are naked, that they are unabashed cries of joy, frustration, pain, and awe to the God who sacrificed His Son on the cross so nothing would ever come between us and Him again.

Henri Nouwen writes, *"The more we dare to reveal our whole trembling self to [God], the more we will be able to sense that His love, which is perfect love, casts out all our fears."*[1]

Naked prayer leads us to a greater experience of God's love because there is nothing more to separate us from it—not pretense nor pride, not dressed up fancy words nor covered up distractions. Naked prayer bares the most vulnerable aspects of our souls to God's overwhelming, all-consuming tenderness. It allows us to be exposed—yet never ashamed—before the Lifter of our heads. I can't think of a better reason to take a shower.

- How has your concept of prayer been influenced and developed through the years?

- How does it feel to think of being naked, unrehearsed, and unpolished before God?

- Do you trust the love of God to accept and embrace your vulnerabilities?

Dear Almighty God, there are times when I allow my worries, shame, fear, and pride to come between us. I don't want that, and I'm grateful You don't want it either. Teach me vulnerability, Lord. Allow me the gift of nakedness before You, that the most delicate, tender aspects of my heart are healed and made strong in Your love. May my trust in Your forgiveness, Your tenderness, and Your grace grow, so that our communion is rich and deep and

flourishing. May my prayers reflect the truth of who

I am and the magnificence of who You are. I want

so much to know You and to be known by You.

Make it so, my Abba.

Amen.

9.

The Sheep of His Pasture

*"My sheep listen to my voice; I know them,
and they follow me. I give them eternal life,
and they shall never perish;
no one will snatch them out of my hand."*
—John 10:27–28

Last summer my kids and I attended our first official State Fair. I've been a city girl my whole life, so this was an entirely new adventure for all three of us. Walking through the gate was like falling into a chapter of *Charlotte's Web*. A combined aroma of butter, barbeque, and manure filled the air. There were carnival barkers and stilt walkers and men wearing cowboy hats who actually looked like they might be cowboys. I'd never seen so many farm animals in one place. I discovered how many foods can be deep-fried and placed on a stick—everything from pickles to Twinkies.

We went into the "Beef" building and walked around long rows of cows available for purchase. We stopped and looked at a large black cow grazing in a stall. My daughter, Elizabeth, asked the farmer nearby the cow's name. "Uh, we don't give them names since we use them for ..." My eyes pleaded with him not to go any further. Seeing my desperation, the farmer's words trailed off, and he suddenly got very busy rearranging hay. My daughter did not need to know these cows would be an upcoming family meal, not the next family pet.

We wandered over to a large arena where about 25 sheep were kept in a pen off to the side. An announcer roared, "The mutton run will begin in five minutes! Get your seats now!"

We had no idea what a mutton run was, but the

excitement in his voice told us we shouldn't miss the opportunity to find out. We bounded into the metal bleachers and got settled just in time for the festivities to begin.

"Ladies and gentlemen, welcome to the Mid-County State Fair mutton run!" barked the announcer. "This one's for the kids! There is a balloon duct-taped to the hindquarter of six different sheep. If you can grab that balloon off a sheep, you win a prize! Kids, come on down and try your hand at mutton running!"

About 30 kids clamored down the bleachers to take part, and they were quickly divided up into age groups and placed at the far end of the arena. The first contest was ready to begin.

The gate opened and about 15 sheep were let into the arena, including the unfortunate souls with balloons taped to their bottoms. The kids sprang into action. The sheep, seeing 10 wild-eyed kids hurtling toward them, took off running. The crowd jumped to its feet.

Now, I'm not saying the sheep had no reason to run; after all, those kids were unhinged with excitement. But man oh man, those sheep lost their minds with confusion and fear! If one would start to run in a particular direction, the others would follow, pushing into one another in a desperate attempt to find safety in numbers. Watching the colored balloons bob up and down on the butts of the sheep was both hilarious and slightly horrifying. Parents were screaming instructions to their kids, as if anyone could hear anything in the melee.

The crowd roared.

The kids ran.

The sheep panicked.

In about four minutes, all of the balloons were grabbed. The kids were dirty and happy. The sheep were unharmed. The mutton run was over. Prizes were distributed, kids reunited with their parents, and most of the crowd made a quick exit. My kids and I stayed behind, curious to see what would happen with the sheep still in the arena.

The owner of the sheep swung the gate to their pen wide open. The rest of their sheep friends were there waiting for them.

Only the sheep would not go easily.

They were still running and bumping into one another, and they didn't even notice safety was just steps away. They would run right past the open gate to a corner, bunched up and backed into a dead end. Then they would take off in the opposite direction. The opening to their pen was large—more than eight feet across—but it made no difference to the sheep. Just because a safe passage had been offered didn't mean the sheep were going to take it.

It took the rancher far longer to get the sheep back into the pen than it had for the kids to capture the balloons. He spoke softly to them. His movements were slow so they would not startle. For someone who looked tough, he was surprisingly gentle. He would get behind the sheep to encourage them forward. He would move around to their side so they didn't get separated. He would circle them, back and forth, ahead and behind, herding them ever so patiently in the right direction. Had they just trusted their master, the sheep would have found sanctuary swiftly. Instead, they required calling and cajoling.

My goodness, it was tedious. Those sheep went in every direction except where their master was inviting them to go. They chose the illusion of safety bunched up in a corner or running at full speed rather than the true peace of their pen. They didn't listen to his soothing voice. They bleated and baaahhhed to one another instead. They stayed afraid long after there was anything to fear.

And you know what? There was really nothing for them to be scared of in the first place. The sheep outweighed those kids by at least 100 pounds. Those 4-year-olds weren't even after the sheep—they were after the balloons. The sheep's master allowed for the mutton run to take place, but he knew all along they could not be snatched from him. He wouldn't have allowed that.

As I watched this all unfold that day at the state fair, I remembered how Jesus describes Himself and how He describes me: *"I am the good shepherd; I know my sheep and my sheep know me—just as the Father knows me and I know the Father—and I lay down my life for the sheep."* (John 10:14–15)

This life we live is going to duct-tape plenty of balloons to our behinds, and sometimes we cannot help ourselves but run. Most of our troubles make little sense. Some of our experiences are terrifying. But the Shepherd is there—calling us, sometimes cajoling, always patiently leading us home. He encircles us with His love and offers us a respite from all the running and all those dead ends.

I'm a city girl. I had never seen a bunch of sheep in action. Yet that day I realized more than ever that to be called "the sheep of His pasture" is not exactly a nod to my wits and courage, if you know what I mean. The shoe (or hoof, rather) fits more than I'd like, but that's okay. I'll be a sheep if that means I get to be His.

- How do you react to fear? Do you run? Do you look for safety in numbers?

- In the midst of confusion, what opportunities for shelter have you overlooked?

- Have you slowed down enough lately to listen to and know the Shepherd's voice?

Oh Master, may I hear Your voice above the melee.
May I remember that even if I am frightened, there
is nothing to fear. You are with me. You are guarding
and guiding my life. And when I've backed myself
into a corner, I pray I remember the undeniable truth
of Your goodness, Your faithfulness, and Your
protection. You encircle me, back and forth and
ahead and behind, herding me ever so patiently in
the right direction. I am a sheep of Your pasture,
and I am Yours. In You I trust. In You I rejoice.
In You, I am home.
Amen.

10.

Minor Scrapes

"Are not five sparrows sold for two pennies?
Yet not one of them is forgotten by God."
—Luke 12:6

Recently it occurred to me that I regularly weigh and measure the joys and trials of my life based on whether or not they are worth sharing with someone else. Plenty of predicaments are big enough to talk, pray, and lament about to no less than three girlfriends. But the small stuff? I relegate those little gems to social media. And even those items go through a filtering system. Is my recent fender bender post-worthy? Is it an interesting tidbit that will weave my "friends" and me together in the common bond of the human experience, or is it simply embarrassing? Will it garner comments, or worst of all, will it be ignored entirely?

Generally, the largest, hardest parts of my life typically don't get posted on social media. But man, oh man, they get prayed over. Sometimes these are desperate, groveling, 17-snotty-tissues types of prayers. Other times they are prayers filled with thanksgiving and praise. Then there are the other items: the incidental experiences and feelings I have ... the minutiae I don't think really matters. I save those for quick and quirky social media posts and nothing more. Reason being, I hold the underlying attitude that I don't like to bother God with the small stuff.

Then I remember who Abba is.

He's the One who counts the hairs on our heads. He goes after one measly lost sheep. He knows when a sparrow falls from the sky. And He recognizes the beauty of two pennies offered by a poor widow.

Seems like He might like the small stuff after all.

When a child skins his knee, he doesn't keep it to himself. He does not play judge and jury to his wound. Instead, he runs pell-mell into the arms of a parent who will ooh and aah over him, inspect the injury, and decide the course of treatment. Most likely, the parent will kiss the top of the child's head and give him a big hug. If the child is really lucky, he'll get a Band-aid. And what usually happens? With his scrape properly acknowledged, his hurt properly comforted, and his confidence properly returned, he's off and running toward the next adventure.

Hopefully, none of us is regularly separating what is "prayer-worthy" and what is "post-worthy." But I suspect that, like me, there are times when we do.

God wants all of us: the minor scrape and the major wound; the stubbed toe and the broken heart. He is the Healer of all. Sometimes we need major surgery.

Other times, we need a kiss on the forehead and a few words of comfort; then we're on our feet again. Who are we to decide what is important to God? He chose the weak things to confound the strong. He chose the foolish things to shame the wise. And He cares about the sparrow.

Everything matters to Him.

- Are there small matters in your life that you've kept to yourself instead of bringing them to God?

- What minor scrapes in your life need a kiss from your Abba today?

Dear Abba, sometimes I am embarrassed at the thoughts that weigh on my mind. They seem so trivial, so meaningless—especially when I compare

them to my most pressing needs and the needs of this world. I know I should bring it all to You, but sometimes my "all" is kind of weird. It's kind of ... I don't know ... small. But if, as Scripture says, You like the poor and the weak and even the little sparrow, then maybe You are more interested in the details of my life than I imagine. I'm sorry for the times I've withheld the small scrapes in my life that hurt, even if they aren't big or consequential. Will You show me Your comfort in all my circumstances, in both the major and minor details? In Your hands, everything matters. I offer it all to You.

Amen.

11.

Choice by Choice

*"Run for dear life from evil;
hold on for dear life to good."*
—Romans 12:9 (MSG)

I was a big fan of *Breaking Bad*, the AMC television series starring Bryan Cranston as Walter White. I watched every episode with a mixture of horror and rapt attention bordering on addiction. In the series finale, as the camera pulled away from the final shot of Walter, I felt both sad and relieved. Sadness—that there would not be any more episodes to marvel at for the incomparable writing, cinematography, and acting. Relief—that I would not have to watch a man continue to self-destruct (and cause the destruction of so many around him) right before my eyes. I'm not sure it can be qualified as a "happy ending," but it sure was a good one.

Walter White has been described by critics, bloggers, and journalists as an "anti-hero." He was a middle-class, mild-mannered, and slightly geeky high school chemistry teacher who, over a period of two years, became a drug lord and murderer. How does that happen? Slowly.

Walter starts out being a guy whom many of us can relate to. He was a family man who worked hard and worried about money and providing for his kids. Some of his dreams for his life didn't quite work out how he had hoped.

Then Walter was diagnosed with cancer—and he decided to take control of a life that was slipping through his fingers. So began his descent. There were times along the way that I didn't want to relate to Walter so much anymore. Like when he let a young girl overdosing on heroin die before his eyes.

Or when he lied so continually and convincingly to his wife and family. Or when he killed a friend simply because he had hurt Walter's pride. In those moments, most of me stopped relating to Walter.

Most of me.

But when I'm honest, there is a niggling thought lying at the base of my brain that wonders if I really am so different from Walter.

Walter didn't "break bad" overnight. A thousand small decisions along the way led to that final parting shot on the series finale. Walter didn't lie, let people die, and kill in autonomous moments. He went step by step, thought by thought, choice by choice, down his road to destruction—all the while justifying his choices with reasons that made sense to him. Like the cancer growing inside his body, Walter metastasized slowly.

When I think about my own steps, thoughts, and

choices, I feel closer to Walter than I prefer. I can justify my actions that have no business being justified. I have never been a drug lord or committed murder. I try to live an honest, moral life. But there are times when I've allowed relationships to die right before my eyes because I didn't want to experience the pain of working through them. I have had promptings in my spirit that I've chosen to ignore or let die because I lacked the faith to obey God when He called.

Walter White had a thousand small opportunities to adjust his ways, to turn back on his path, and to make things right. He chose not to. God offers us the same choice. It's utterly terrifying, isn't it? We can choose to absolutely ruin our lives if we want to.

But we also have the choice to give our lives to Christ, and in a thousand small opportunities along the way, we are offered a life of redemption and abundance. No matter how much we've blown it, the riches of God's grace will always outnumber our failings, and a full, beautiful life is always possible.

Hope is a consistent offering.

Step by step, we can live by faith—even when we are mystified by what God is doing. Thought by thought, we can replace destructive thinking with the words and promises of Scripture. Choice by choice, we can invest in friends who inspire and encourage, families that love and need us, and our God who has redeemed and is redeeming us from all the ways we "break bad." It's the best happy ending of all.

- Are there choices you've been making that are sinful, metastasizing your relationship with God and others?

- Knowing that it is never too late to turn around, do you desire to make a change toward God and away from evil?

- If so, make today the day that will be different—step by step, thought by thought, choice by choice. With God's grace, love, and power, hope is a consistent offering.

Dear Abba, This life offers so many choices. I don't always make the right ones. Sometimes it's out of ignorance, and sometimes it's just a mistake. Then there are times when I am either thoughtless, careless, or just plain rebellious. I make decisions out of fear, faithlessness, anger, or envy. In those moments, will You pierce my consciousness with Your Holy Spirit? Will You remind me who You are and who I am in You? I'm grateful You discipline those You love. You are watching out for me, and I know You want the best for me. I ask for Your protection, Your guidance, and Your will in my life, thought by thought, step by step, little choice by little

choice, that I will grow in wisdom and grace,

ever becoming more reflective of You.

Amen.

12.

Rushing Rivers

"Be still, and know that I am God."
—Psalm 46:10

Sometimes I long for the movement of life to just stop for a while. That hasn't happened yet, but a girl can hope, right? I yearn for a smooth, quiet-pond life, but what I have is more like a rushing river. It's the same for all of us; life doesn't stay still for anyone. There are ripples and waves, deep waters and shallow edges, rough rapids and a few smooth stretches. The current slows or speeds up depending on the season and the direction of its flow. No matter what, it's always moving.

Whether we feel confident about it, afraid of it, or

maybe a bit of both, change always arrives. Waters will soon shift, and all that is before us right now will be different. The key is to stay still in the midst of the madness, or every new occurrence has the potential to carry us away. We need to plant our feet, adjust our stance, and look around a bit, exactly where we stand. By spending too much time in the future or regretting what we did or didn't do in the past, we ignore the unique opportunities of today.

As I write this, my son, Cole, is preparing to leave home for college. It will create a whitewater shift in our household. I picture Cole walking into his dorm room, and my heart wants to rip in two. This is a good change, I know that. But it's hard. Cole has not stayed stagnant for one moment of his life. He has changed every day since he was born. I kept asking him to slow down, but he refused. (Apparently we raised a rebel.)

Yes, it's all moving so quickly. But even a rushing river is consistent in its ability to offer refreshment.

Even rapids have a cadence. Close friendships, a supportive spouse, the dog who greets you with enthusiasm at the end of the day—all offer reassurance that some things, like river banks, are solid enough to rely on. They are not completely immovable, but they are firm enough to keep the river from running roughshod over us.

And the most reliable and unchanging of all? God Himself. Jesus Christ is the same yesterday, today, and forever. He is solid ground when everything else becomes shifting sand. He is timeless. But because we are not, the present is the only place we are together with God in the same space. He is always right here. When we remain still and focused despite the rush all around us, we are witnesses to God's movement as it occurs.

When we read Psalm 46, we see a montage of chaos: the earth melting, mountains falling, shields burning, and waters roaring. And what does the Lord tell His people to do with all of the mayhem? "*Be still, and know that I am God,"* He says. In other words, God is here, and that's what matters most.

When we are still before God, we are awakened to the abundance of the here and now. The sacred unfolds before our eyes. Consequently, we are blessed with unique moments of intimacy not only with God but with others because we are attentive enough to recognize the importance of the moment.

Next week, Cole will be living in another state. For now, he is still roaming around the house, rifling through the refrigerator, and asking me what is for dinner. I'm going to soak up every moment.

Change keeps coming. By this time next week, life will be different. Feelings, thoughts, interactions, and opportunities here today will be carried away by the current before we know it. In all our circumstances, we are invited to stay still, embrace what will be gone soon enough, and find peace in our ever-present, unchanging God.

- What parts of your life are rushing by quickly?

- Does the idea of being still in the midst of chaos sound daunting or refreshing?

- How can you be still before God today?

Dear Lord, everything is moving so swiftly. I get a bit overwhelmed by the changes that come my way. Sometimes I focus on regrets of the past or worries about the future. When I long for things to slow down, help me to long even more deeply for Your presence right where I am. Open my eyes, my ears, and my heart to what You are doing in this precise moment. Still my mind, that I can experience You. Calm my heart and attune my soul to stay planted, firm, and secure, where I am, which is where You are.

Amen.

13.

Inspired

*"Therefore encourage one another
and build each other up,
just as in fact you are doing."*
—1 Thessalonians 5:11

I haven't been writing much lately. I've been waiting for inspiration.

And waiting.

And waiting.

I have no desire to fill up a page with words that "will do" when they really don't. To a creative mind, inspiration is a valued and rare gift. We wait on it like an awkward teen hoping to be noticed by the school hottie. Author and speaker Elizabeth Gilbert calls this type of inspiration "elusive and tantalizing."[1]

While I've been waiting for this elusive and tantalizing inspiration, I spent time with my friend Amy, who is a breast cancer survivor. I had dinner with Kristin and Diane, who have both cared for and recently buried parents with Alzheimer's. I had breakfast with Nancy, who ministers to women with unwanted pregnancies. I saw Mindy, who has been plagued with medical issues while caring for her young children. I chatted with Ellen and Norma, who both started businesses that were born out of passion and talent. I've spent time with people who chose the hard thing, the faithful thing, the loving thing, when most people would do the exact opposite.

It's only dawned on me now that while I've been waiting for inspiration to hit, I've had countless opportunities to be inspired.

Elusive inspiration happens *to* us. It can arrive like a

tidal wave or a whisper. When we look inward for it, it may or may not be there. Days might stretch out before us in one long, beige streak of monotony while we wait. Inspiration is fickle; it comes and goes as it pleases, and it refuses to be controlled.

But to *be* inspired? That is done on purpose. It's never elusive. However, it requires our attention. We are surrounded by sunrises and sunsets and birds that sing and music and babies and laughter and hugs and great food and great wine. It's all ours for the taking. (Well, you might have to pay for the food and wine.) We just have to notice it.

Then there are the people. People take a bit more time and attentiveness than a sunset, but they are an even deeper well of inspiration. We can learn their stories and hear their triumphs and heartbreaks, and we will be reminded that beautiful, broken people are doing beautiful, brave things in this life. From people, we will remember that we are not alone on the journey. We can draw courage from their strength and fortitude even if they would never describe themselves as courageous. (Courageous people rarely do.)

Whether you are a writer or a CEO, an accountant or a blackjack dealer, your heart needs regular exposure to inspiration. It fuels us. It animates us. It motivates us to live boldly. Rather than simply waiting for it, let's go after it.

Seek out the people God has already placed in your life. Ask them about themselves, then listen expectantly to their answers. Discover courage and strength in their stories. Allow yourself to be moved by their struggles and encouraged by their triumphs. Find common connection and weave your heart with theirs. You will no longer need to wait for inspiration; you will find it right there in the person standing in front of you. And when you do, let that person know they inspire you. You just might inspire them back.

- Who inspires you to live with courage and faith?

- Whose story might you be able to learn this week?

- How can you serve as an inspiration to others?

Dear Lord, sometimes I try to rely on myself too much. I turn inward for inspiration when what I really need to do is look around and find it in the examples of others. Bring people into my life who inspire, challenge, and teach me how to live well. Remind me to seek out and learn people's stories, so that my compassion for them grows. Let the care and connection I experience with them deepen my experience of You. Thank You for surrounding me

every day with sunrises, sunsets, birds, babies, and laughter. May I learn to pay attention to all of it. Most especially, thank You for giving me the opportunity to seek out Your people. May I lean in and listen well and find inspiration in their experiences. I pray that my life is a humble reflection of Your beauty, love, and grace and that in witnessing it, others may be inspired too.

Amen.

14.

The Value of a Widget

*" 'For my thoughts are not your thoughts,
neither are your ways my ways,' declares the LORD."*
—Isaiah 55:8

I love to watch those television shows that feature pawnbrokers and the astonishing items people bring into their shops to sell—all kinds of rare, historical, whimsical, or just plain bizarre items that have been purchased at garage sales or kept in a family for generations. Sometimes folks just want to make a few bucks; other times they are hoping for a major chunk of change. No matter how much money the seller desires, it's up to the pawnbroker to determine the actual worth of the book, painting, gun, instrument, or other odd widget set before them.

Many times, people have a fairly accurate sense of what their item is worth, and a deal is struck quickly. Once in a while, a person will walk in with an old book they got for a buck at a garage sale, only to discover it's worth $5,000. On the other hand, sometimes people will have what they believe is an extremely valuable item, only to have the appraiser break the news that the item they are hoping is worth a small fortune is, in fact, a replica, imitation, or forgery of the real widget they thought they owned.

It is these folks who interest me the most. When they figure out they've been lugging around, for example, a fake Civil War sword for the past 30 years, through nine moves, four states, and two marriages, the reaction varies. Some walk away, defeated. Others argue and insist that the appraiser—the one who is an expert in Civil War weapons—is just plain wrong. It doesn't matter that the sword in question was actually mass produced in

1979—to the owner, in their perspective, it is valuable beyond measure. They leave the shop with their possession in hand, determined to find the right buyer who will value their (non)Civil War sword as much as they do. Facts don't matter—the feeling or belief they have about their item is all that motivates them.

Like kitchen appliances, winter jackets, and old paperbacks we carry from home to home with us, the ideas, stories, and perspectives we hold on to need to be re-evaluated every so often. We need to take them off that dusty shelf of our past and inspect them for flaws. Maybe we've clung to a belief about ourselves or about God that, when inspected closely, is a twisting or a forgery of the truth found in Scripture.

Maybe our faith has deepened, our understanding has expanded, or our experiences have taught us that life is not what we thought it once was. If we are being transformed by the renewing of our minds

(Romans 12:2) and sanctified by the Holy Spirit, then hopefully we are not the same as we were some years ago. Maybe we are finally beginning to understand the enormity of God's grace, so the self-criticism we once believed motivated us to "improve" doesn't make sense anymore. Maybe our experience of God's peace and provision has developed in times of scarcity, and we no longer connect our sense of security with the ability to pay the bills. Maybe our ideas about marriage, kids, and career are transforming in light of having (or not having) them.

How many worthless or wrong ideas do we hang on to only because they were handed down from generation to generation? How many insignificant widgets have we clung to? What beliefs and thought patterns have shown themselves to be not only worthless, but damaging? Perhaps our hands and hearts have been so busy clutching onto the familiar-yet-worthless that they cannot open up to the gifts

God has that are real, true, and far more precious.

Today is a day to take inventory of what is truly valuable. It's a new day to clean out thoughts of self-condemnation. It's time to question false ideas about God—that He is mad, impatient, or just putting up with us. Today we can let go of judging others because at one time it made us feel safe, in control, or falsely confident. Today we can question what we were told about ourselves by people who didn't really know us or seek to encourage us.

We are the curators of what takes up space on the bookshelves of our minds. Hopefully we are always growing, deepening, and widening our under-standing of God. I pray we each become experts at differentiating the true joy found only in Jesus Christ from the counterfeit offered in so many other places. As our confidence in the Savior increases, we can look at worn-out ideas and old patterns for what they are: things that we once thought were valuable, but in reality, are not. With the renewing of our minds and the gentleness of the One who has saved us and is always transforming us, may we discover new volumes of God's peace and love found in the truth of His Word and in the beauty of His unending daily grace.

- What thoughts have you carried around about yourself that are a forgery of God's truth?

- What old patterns might God be inviting you to let go of in order to discover new volumes of His grace and peace?

Oh Lord, I'm grateful You are an expert in understanding what is valuable. Help me let go of my tight grip on what is familiar and comfortable in favor of what is true. Show me what is worth keeping and what needs to be thrown away. Let me

recognize the truth from the counterfeit notions I

have lived with for so long I never thought to

appraise their value. May I look to the Bible for

guidance—because it's Your distinct love shown on

the pages of Your Word that has given my life the

only value that matters.

Amen.

15.

The Sparrow Flies Free

"The LORD sets prisoners free ..."
—Psalm 146:7

I am free.

I am no longer held captive by circumstance.

The storms may blow

the lightning flash

the thunder clap

the rain pour down.

Whatever comes ...

I am

unendingly secure

tightly held

deeply known

fervently loved

and abundantly free.

I am free

from wondering if I will lose God's love.

I am free

from worrying He is not with me.

I am free

from the need to control things.

Because

God is in control

He wants good things for me.

I am free

from harsh expectations of myself and others.

I am no longer held captive by

doubt

control

expectation

sin.

Because

Jesus Christ opened the cage door

and removed it from the hinges.

Even if

I fly back into the cage myself

Even when

I have built a very nice nest there

I am not locked in.

At any time

I can leave the confines of those bars

and enjoy the open air.

Because

in Jesus Christ, I am free.

I am free.

16.

Diagnosis: Undefined

"You know me inside and out, you know every bone in my body; You know exactly how I was made, bit by bit, how I was sculpted from nothing into something. Like an open book, you watched me grow from conception to birth; all the stages of my life were spread out before you, the days of my life all prepared before I'd even lived one day."
—Psalm 139:13–16 (MSG)

My first pregnancy was not a smooth one. We didn't know whether or not the child growing inside of me was going to be healthy. Test results were contradictory, and my husband, Danny, and I were left to wait and wonder, praying for the best yet preparing for the worst.

Our daughter, Elizabeth, was born almost six weeks

early. She weighed 4 pounds, 12 ounces. She had difficulty nursing and cried a lot. By the time she was 3, we learned that she had an odd assortment of genetic characteristics. Her doctors knew something was wrong, but they didn't know exactly what it was. Danny and I were increasingly frustrated with the lack of answers.

We knew our daughter had speech problems and other developmental delays. If only we could find a diagnosis for her condition. We needed definitive answers to our questions about the subtle but undeniable differences between Elizabeth and other children. I hated repeatedly having to explain to doctors and educators why we were requesting their services.

My little girl simply couldn't be categorized, which was extremely difficult because I always prefer order and organization. I longed for a book, support group, or website that would address my concerns—then I would know how to handle my daughter based on others' previously paved paths.

Furthermore, a diagnosis would have made it easier for Elizabeth to receive educational services, and doctors would not have had to repeatedly test her and experiment with different medical theories.

If only we had a specific response to the question, "Does your daughter have any known medical condition?", then Elizabeth's characteristics could be included in one profound medical depiction.

When Elizabeth began early intervention classes, we learned about many other special needs children. Through being exposed to the medical conditions of these children, we realized how shortsighted we'd been in wanting a pat diagnosis for Elizabeth.

Over the years, we have learned there are benefits to not labeling our daughter. Every doctor and therapist with whom she interacts really has to learn about *her*. She fits no mold—so she can be viewed as God intended each of us to be seen: as an individual who should never be summed up in a label or diagnosis.

Elizabeth, therefore, is not defined by her medical deficits. Her physical disabilities might make some people feel sorry for her. But her sense of humor, fearlessness, strong will, and nurturing instincts make Elizabeth a unique, intricate, fully developed and three-dimensional human being who brings tremendous joy to those around her.

In the Bible, there are countless stories of those who wanted to find nice, neat, little boxes for other people. They wanted a diagnosis, a word to sum up the totality of another so they wouldn't have to do the work of actually learning about them. They used words such as *sinner, adulterer, paralytic,* or *demon-possessed* in order to dismiss those different from themselves. They thought Jesus should categorize people by their heritage (*those darn Samaritans*), their occupation (*a tax collector! ugh!*), or their sins (*doesn't He know that the woman washing His feet is a sinner?*). But Jesus wasn't interested in packing boxes. He was interested in people. He looked into their eyes (their souls, really), searched their hearts, asked them questions, talked to them, and touched them. If anything, He obliterated the boxes.

None of us should be labeled; we should not be restricted by descriptions and diagnoses. But sometimes out of fear, past experience, or convenience, we try to cram people into little spaces because it takes time and hard work to understand people different than we are.

Relating to my daughter has exposed my own need to define others. It isn't my proudest attribute—but I'm learning. Because I'm unable to categorize my little girl, who is now grown up, I've had to give up expectations of her capabilities and complexities. Instead, I've been given the gift of learning about her—one day at a time. I am delighted and disappointed, surprised and challenged, elated and frustrated every day.

Each one of us is alive—complex and complicated, not designed to conform to another's idea of where we should fit. Elizabeth should not be judged by her deficits any more than each of us should be summed up merely by our job, marital status, best achievements, or worst mistakes. Let's obliterate the boxes we've created for one another—as well as the ones we've created for ourselves.

Our true "diagnosis"—the only one that really counts—is that we are beloved children of God. Everything else is secondary.

- Are there actions or events in your life that have caused you to define yourself in unkind, narrow ways?

- How comfortable are you with people different from yourself—not just developmentally delayed people, but anyone who is different from you in looks, religion, political views, lifestyle, or background?

- What boxes need to be obliterated in your life?

Dear Abba, You know exactly how I was sculpted from nothing into something—because You are my Creator. I am adopted, forgiven, embraced, and beloved by You. May I define myself first and foremost by this unshakable fact. I depend upon You to guide, challenge, and quicken me in order to see others as You do. Help me to obliterate the boxes that form so quickly when I don't understand or relate to someone else. Help me to learn from and enjoy those different from me. Grow my heart, expand my mind, and open my arms to embrace

and celebrate them. Above all, may I treat others as

I want to be treated. And may I celebrate the

complexity and beauty of every individual heart

You've created, including my own.

Amen.

17.

Postcards & Precipices

"I keep asking that the God of our Lord Jesus Christ, the glorious Father, may give you the Spirit of wisdom and revelation, so that you may know him better. I pray that the eyes of your heart may be enlightened in order that you may know the hope to which he has called you, the riches of his glorious inheritance in his holy people, and his incomparably great power for us who believe."
—Ephesians 1:17–19

Most of us have seen pictures of the Grand Canyon from the time we were kids. Depictions of this cavernous natural wonder are everywhere—on calendars and screen savers, in doctor's office paintings, on souvenir magnets, postcards, and T-shirts. Familiar to us in everything from plastic snow globes to wall murals, we know what it looks like. So when my family decided to visit there, I thought I knew what to expect.

It was late afternoon when I first saw the actual Grand Canyon.

This is the point in the story when I should describe how taken aback I was by seeing one of the seven natural wonders of the world for the first time. I should share how amazed I was at its grandeur and majesty. I should say that I got tears in my eyes and was overtaken by humbled emotion. But that is not what happened.

As I stood there looking out at the Grand Canyon, I waited to be overwhelmed by the beauty of it all. But what I actually felt was ... indifference. I had seen the pictures and read the brochures, and now I was standing before the real thing. Yep, it's what I expected. Big hole. A lot of rocks.

We left the park that evening and stayed at a nearby hotel. The next morning, we set out to spend the entire day exploring at the Grand Canyon. This time, we went out to the far railings and walked a trail along the edge of the canyon. I began to notice some interesting details that caught me by surprise.

The layers of rock were subtly different from one another in color and texture. Some places at the bottom of the canyon were plentiful with trees, while other areas were barren. There were sheer drop-offs shoulder to shoulder with gradual declines along the rim. Even the skyline looked different depending on where I was standing. The wind howled fiercely at one lookout, but at another it was perfectly still. There were crags, crevices, pillars, and buttes that varied in height, depth, and formation. The air was crisp, and the gravel under my feet crunched when I walked. Now I wasn't just looking at the Grand Canyon; I was inside of and experiencing it.

The postcard images in my mind dissipated with

every cold gust of wind and warm sunlit rock that I encountered. The more I explored the Grand Canyon, the bigger it got. It was only after walking around inside the real thing that I felt humbled and awestruck by its enormity. I needed to not just look at it; I needed to be *enveloped* by it.

Because I had seen pictures and postcards, I thought I knew what the Grand Canyon looked like. But I was so satisfied with replicas that I almost missed taking in the real thing. My heart began to see for the first time what my eyes thought they had already understood.

We can do that with God's love, too. We can be so satisfied with a velvet painting of Jesus that we miss out on experiencing the real One. Sometimes we are so sure we already know what He looks like that we don't recognize Him when He's standing right in front of us.

We get easily distracted by things that offer a

reflection of His love—such as church, Bible studies, friends, and family—that we miss the blessing of what those things point to: the source of love Himself.

And sometimes, if we're honest, we prefer our imitation versions of Jesus more than the real thing because we can hold (that is, control) "plastic-souvenir-shop" Jesus. We can keep Him where we want Him and, truthfully, we like that, because we know that the real Jesus offers an uneven path of crunchy rocks, sharp edges, and sudden drops. The real Jesus will allow the winds to howl in the midst of breathtaking beauty. The real Jesus is dangerous. Sometimes the real Jesus doesn't line up with who we think He should be, and maybe we are afraid of that, so we satisfy ourselves with a two-dimensional "flat Stanley" kind of God when what we really need is to be enveloped by His very real magnificence.

Each one of us is invited to be amazed and undone by Jesus Christ. We don't need to be content with snow-globed safety (or worse, indifference) when we can live awestruck by and inside of the genuine love, hope, and power of the Lord. But for that to happen, we have to walk around a bit, explore, and discover the truth of who He is. Could we lose our life in the process? Yes. Will we gain much more if we do? You bet.

It's only when we are standing in real places, in spite of (and maybe because of) any possible danger, that we experience awe. Safety will not produce authenticity.

Being satisfied with readily available, humanly constructed cheap imitations causes us to miss the majesty, glory, and unrelenting beauty of what God offers. Sometimes we get so busy in the gift shop looking for postcards that we miss the actual experience.

The intimate details, the sounds, the colors, and the wind on my face crystallized the difference between a paper facsimile and the true depth, height, and immensity of the Grand Canyon. Daily I want to realize this with Jesus as well—to know Him in an intimate, experiential, and deep way.

Without recognizing the glory of its brilliant Creator, even the Grand Canyon itself is really just a big hole and a lot of rocks.

The love of Jesus is wide and long and high and deep, and it's real and right in front of you; He's ready for relationship. My challenge: Live in awe of what you discover there, and may you never be satisfied with anything less.

- When is it tempting for you to settle for a plastic-souvenir Jesus instead of the real thing?

- Are there areas in your relationship with God where you have grown indifferent?

- When was the last time you experienced awe?

Dear Jesus, forgive me for the times I've settled for safe, controllable ideas of You rather than a genuine relationship grounded in vulnerability and trust. Reveal to me the places in my life where I have mistaken cheap imitations of Your love for Your genuine truth. Oh Lord, renew in me a sense of awe for You. Help me to once again (or maybe for the first time) experience how wide and long and high and deep is Your love for me. May I embrace Your beauty as well as Your danger. Allow me to not only see You, but to be enveloped by You. Let me never become indifferent to Your voice, Your presence, Your beauty, Your majesty.

Amen.

18

Hope, of All Things

"We have this hope as an anchor for the soul,
firm and secure."
—Hebrews 6:19

Though I consider myself to be one, I am quite suspicious of happy Christians. I secretly (and a tad condescendingly) wonder if really happy people are ignoring their inner pain or are a bit simple minded, blissfully unaware of the difficulties this life has to offer. When someone responds to any question with "God is good!" or other pat phrases, all kinds of red flags go up. I wonder if he or she is sincere or trying to impress me (or worse yet, God).

Over the course of my early life, I spent a long time

trying to manage my worries, doubts, anger, and sadness on my own. This led to shame and depression. When I came to understand that we have a God who invites us to a life of honesty instead of emotional tidiness, it changed everything. I learned to trust Him with all of my frailties, including a heart that regularly loses hope and a mind that wanders into the dark regions of doubt and despair.

My embarrassingly vulnerable relationship with God has been the single most transformative thing in my life. It would cheapen His grace to pretend I've got it together. So this is the reason why I'm a little suspicious of those who can summarize their faith with a phrase that fits onto a bumper sticker.

But I've learned that just because someone is happy doesn't mean they are glossing over the anguish, injustice, and evil in this world. And when a person is hopeful, it doesn't mean they don't have a reason to despair.

Sometimes the seeds of hope grow in the soil of unbelievable pain.

Let me tell you about a couple I know.

Katherine Wolf was 26 years old and married to the love of her life, Jay. She was a new mom of their 6-month-old son, James. She was vibrant, with a strong faith in God, and she was strikingly beautiful to boot. Happiness was a regular part of life for Jay and Katherine. In one completely unforeseen moment, however, everything changed when Katherine suffered a massive brain stem stroke that should have killed her.

Miraculously, she lived.

But the stroke deeply affected her body, her marriage, her faith, and her way of life. She spent two months in a coma and a year in rehabilitation. She was unable to hold up her own head, let alone care for her infant son. She had to relearn to speak, walk, and swallow. Jay was thrust into circumstances that threatened to remove any shred of happiness he once enjoyed with his wife.

It's been seven years since Katherine's stroke. She is permanently paralyzed on one side. She is deaf in one ear. She is blind in one eye. Jay helps her with basic daily tasks like getting dressed and putting on her make-up. But Katherine's vivacious personality and strong spirit are intact. The couple just finished writing their first book. It's about hope, of all things.

I have a tendency to shy away from stories about people who have experienced immense pain with unwavering faith because it makes me feel like a chump in comparison. I mean, really. I complain about a wrong Starbucks order. And I'm supposed to relate to Jay and Katherine?

But while their story is dramatic, this down-to-earth couple is not. They shy away from labels like "heroic." In reading their book *Hope Heals*,[1] I was captivated by their outright ... ordinariness. Instead of feeling intimidated by their faith or somehow worse about my own pettiness, their humor and honesty allow me to connect with them. And isn't connecting with other people's stories part of what knits us together as human beings?

Jay and Katherine's story is uniquely theirs. I wouldn't dare claim to comprehend their immense loss. But in their Southern hospitality and tender humility, they invite us to explore our own journey of faith by sharing theirs. They demonstrate vulnerability with God, and they are honest enough to be vulnerable about God, about their unanswered questions and prayers for Him as well as the healing and hope they've received from Him. They are fiercely faithful people, but somehow they do not wrap up all that has happened to them in a neat, bumper sticker bow so we are left feeling like chumps. My melancholy soul finds deep comfort in their story.

Jay and Katherine Wolf are acutely aware of the difficulties this life holds, yet they radiate a happiness that is real and vibrant. Their hope is genuine and hard-won, and in their book, they generously offer it to the rest of us. Though I still believe they are two of the most heroic people I know, their fragility and transparency impact me most. As I finished the last chapter of their book, I couldn't help but whisper to myself, "God is good."

- Are there certain phrases Christians use that make you feel uneasy?

- How does God offer hope, even when we have reason for despair?

- How might the circumstances of your life serve as a beacon of hope for someone else?

Dear Abba, thank You for Jay, Katherine, and countless others like them who have come up against the worst possible tragedies and somehow become beacons of immeasurable joy and hope in the process. I am simultaneously humbled and inspired by their stories. I'm grateful that You are a God of complexity and that You cannot be summed up in a bumper sticker or catchphrase. Let my hope rest in You when everything else indicates I have a reason to despair. Allow the hardest parts of my life to become a beacon of hope for someone else. You are the One who keeps me secure in stormy waters. You are the anchor for my soul, and I place my faith, trust, and hope in You alone.

Amen.

19.

Alone ... but Not Really

"If I go up to the heavens, you are there;
if I make my bed in the depths, you are there."
—Psalm 139:8

Most of us remember Mary. There are a few Marys discussed in the New Testament. (I bet the name "Mary" made the "Top 10 Baby Names" list in 15 B.C.) But I'm talking about the one who was there from the start. The one most of us know as, "Mary, the mother of God." I wonder if she really felt up to such a lofty title.

If Mary lived in today's world, would she look in the mirror in the morning and give herself a secret wink and a Mona Lisa smile and say, "Hi there, you who are 'favored among women' "? I wonder if she'd be tempted to have a bumper sticker on her car that said, *My son is better than your honor roll student— No, Really!* Would she keep her hands clasped and have a serene look on her face (just like in my nativity set from Costco) when she shopped in crowded malls with her now 3-year-old son in tow?

While Scripture gives us some fascinating glimpses into Mary and a few of her experiences raising Jesus, most of her life is left unrecorded. There is very little information on what she thought of all the events that unfolded during her life. No one knows what it was like to be her.

The same is true for you, me—all of us, actually.

If you chose to write down your life story and included all the details you could possibly think of, it would not properly portray the enormity of the journey, would it? Even the most public parts of your life contain private experiences solely between you and God. The thoughts, emotions, experiences, darkest moments, and highest blessings that have touched your soul will often go beyond words. The essence of who you are and the thoughts and feelings that dwell most deeply in your heart defy describing. In fact, it would cheapen them if we tried. They are yours alone.

Our lives overlap greatly with many other people, and we can be grateful for the shared camaraderie. It is what knits us together as family, friends, fellow sojourners, and human beings in general. But I have those existential moments when it dawns on me that I'm utterly alone in the exact experience of my life.

No one knows precisely what it's like to be me—with my emotions, my experiences, my past, my present. Loneliness can sweep over my soul when I realize that no other human being will ever fully understand or "get" me.

It is a testament to God's creativity that He never

reproduces His works of art. But if we are not vigilant, our uniqueness can invite self-pity and hopelessness. It can isolate us from others and cause us to build a nice little island for ourselves. Even the most intangible parts of our lives are known by our Creator, so we are never truly alone. Not even for a second. Not even for a nanosecond. Every thread of your experience, memory, and emotion has been methodically and purposely woven together by a delicate, strong hand. God desires so strongly that you understand this, He placed His Holy Spirit not around you or beside you but *inside* of you. He sees stuff you'll never see. He knows the groans of your heart even when you don't, and He puts order to your most confused, unintelligible thoughts and emotions.

It's true—no other human being can fully know what it is like to walk in your shoes. But there are many people whom God has placed in your life that *want* to know what it's like. They want to know because they love you, and they need to know because they, too, are hungry for connection. Reach out. Take a chance. Talk about the parts of your life that matter. You will be reminded that as unique as you are, you still have much in common with other souls as hungry for relationship as you. And being assured that God knows all of it, you can have grace for others who only understand part of it.

What was it like to be the mother of God? Only Mary knows for sure. But I hope that along the way, she had a few good girlfriends who laughed with her, cried with her, and knew her well enough. For the rest of it—God was there, and Mary was never alone. The same is true for each of us.

- In what areas of your journey do you feel most alone?

- Have your unique personality and life experiences led you to lean on God, or have they caused you to move toward self-pity or isolation?

- Are you willing to build up a community of people who can know you well enough— even if their knowing is not perfect?

- How can your unique story bring joy and hope to others today?

Dear Abba, my journey in life has been a layered one, hasn't it? So many experiences, so many relationships, so much to remember and contemplate. You've gifted me with extraordinary times of joy and crushing times of pain. You've been there with me in all of it. You've seen it, and You hold it all. Thank You for the unique and complex way You've created me. I pray that my particular

journey leads me to celebrate Your unique calling for my life and steers me away from self-pity or isolation. I want to bring something special into this world You love. I ask that in times of loneliness, my heart will cry out to You for comfort and stability. I need to be reminded that with You, I am never truly alone. And I ask for the courage and strength to share myself with others in ways that connect and grow us, and intertwine our hearts. Thank You for giving me a narrative too complex to ever be described completely. May it reflect the complexity, beauty, and omniscient majesty of You, my Creator, my Life-Giver, my Source, and the Author of my story.

Amen.

20.

An Unexpected Autumn

*"Therefore, if anyone is in Christ, the new creation
has come: The old has gone, the new is here!"*
—2 Corinthians 5:17

Driving home from the party, I kept the radio off. I
was enjoying the silence and was lost in my thoughts
of mundane things, such as what I needed from the
grocery store, my "to-do" list for the following day,
and exactly how many calories were in the bacon-
wrapped date* I had eaten earlier … times seven.

I had been at a dinner party where I wasn't well
known, and though I enjoyed the evening very
much, I left still unsure about where I fit into the
group.

For me, those mundane thoughts on the drive home about the grocery list and those bacon-wrapped dates were nothing short of monumental for me. Here's why. Typically, when I am unsure of the impression I have made on others, I dwell on things I did or said that were, in my critical mind, awkward or weird.

Then I tell myself that I am a social moron.

Then I swear off dinner parties.

Then I declare that I am alone in this world.

Then I go home and eat ice cream.

That didn't happen this time. I simply wondered if we needed milk.

It didn't occur to me until later that my pattern of self-condemning thoughts has begun to change. Yes, I have been intentional about reshaping my destructive self-talk, and yes, I have asked the Lord to transform me in this area. But I didn't think anything was actually happening. Until it did.

Our minds are being renewed at this very moment. Sometimes we don't see it because change can be excruciatingly slow—like watching the leaves on a tree change color. Do we ever really see it happen before our eyes? No. But one day, we look up, and trees that once bloomed with leaves of green are bathed in the warm colors of fall. Just the same, every so often in our journey through life, there comes an unexpected autumn—and we find that transformation is at hand and that God is at work, even when we don't see it coming.

- In reflecting on your journey, what are some "unexpected autumns" of growth and transformation that have taken place?

- Can you see God's hand in the changes that have occurred?

Dear Lord, I'm so grateful that You are always at work, changing, refining, healing, and growing me. Most of the time, the transformation happens so gradually that I don't even notice it until I reflect back on it. Like leaves of green that turn red and gold, new patterns are always forming. Teach me to notice and celebrate the ways You have flooded my life with Your miraculous, transforming work. May Your work be evident to all who know me, that I am a shining example of how You make each one of us new. To You I give all praise, all glory, and all of myself.

Amen.

*There are 58 calories in one bacon-wrapped date—but who's counting, right?

21.

Deeper, Richer, Truer

*"But Jesus often withdrew
to lonely places and prayed."*
—Luke 5:16

Do you get away every once in a while so you can slow down, breathe in and out, and spend some concentrated time, just you and God? I hope so. If Jesus Christ needed it, how much more so do we need it? Going away to contemplate, pray, and seek silence can serve as a sieve for distractions that are too loud, too shallow, or too hectic. Taking a day or two for ourselves might seem like a luxury, but for us to thrive mentally, physically, and spiritually, it is a necessity. It is an opportunity to discover what might be taking up too much of our attention or what we've ignored for far too long. It is a sign of intentional living. And I want to live intentionally, don't you?

Planned time away from normal life allows us to listen for the still, small voice of God. It recalibrates our souls. But after such a time of focus and depth, it's tough to return to everyday life.

When we get back to the strain of our routines and relationships, we are confronted with choices and situations we'd forgotten were there. When we've regained perspective, we have a renewed opportunity to approach our life, thoughts, and God differently. On the other hand, it's easy to slip back into our daily habits and leave the things that developed in our time of rest buried—like a treasure found, then covered back up. Discovered—but not enjoyed. It's true, even our most indelible habits require effort. But changing our focus requires even more concentration.

Learning to live differently in the midst of a life that demands things stay the same requires bravery and intentionality. Purposeful living requires us to bring the sacred into the mundane. It invites us to become uncomfortable in order to find a deeper source of comfort. To live a deeper, richer, truer life, we need to say good-bye to the predictability of the known to make room for the newly discovered.

I believe our souls need time away regularly, and I recommend it highly. But we don't need to wait for a vacation or retreat to practice intentional living. We have everyday opportunities for a deeper, richer, truer life.

We can develop new habits, such as ones that include regular rest and reflection—even if it's just for 10 minutes a day. We can practice presence— when we are not anywhere in our mind other than where our feet are standing. We can find quiet moments of prayer and thanksgiving. We can be mindful of the presence of our Savior in every situation. We can lean in, explore, and ask Him what He has for us in this place, on this day, at this hour. This is the best kind of concentrated effort.

I want so much to live deeply and beautifully. Sometimes I'm not sure I'm very good at it, and I long for time away to get my footing once more. I doubt any of us get this as often as we need it. Let's plan to get away soon, okay? In the meantime, let's explore what's right in front of us. Because God is with us in every moment, we are constantly presented with opportunities to put intentional living into practice. In this moment, let us stand right here, in this quiet or loud or busy or lonely place, and pay attention to the blessings, the peace, and the presence of God within our grasp. What we discover will surely be deep, rich, and true.

- When was the last time you took time away to recalibrate and refresh?

- What kind of life do you believe you are meant to live? How are you demonstrating that?

- How might you practice intentional living this very day?

Dear Abba, there are so many distractions and so many demands on my mind, my time, my heart. How I long to get away and find rest and renewal! Will You open up opportunities for this to happen? In the meantime, will You teach me how to live intentionally in my normal routine? I ask You to help my mind stay clear and focused, seizing every opportunity to pay attention, to be present, and to find Your deeper, richer, truer beauty every day.

Amen.

22.

The Darkness and the Dawn

"… for I have learned in whatever situation I am to be content. I know how to be brought low, and I know how to abound. In any and every circumstance, I have learned the secret of facing plenty and hunger, abundance and need."
—Philippians 4:11–12 (ESV)

My mind stirs before my eyes even open. It's dark in my bedroom. My husband has left for work, and I am in that hazy space between sleep and wakefulness. Thoughts drift in and out; some are ordered and thinking about the day ahead, and some are remnants of the dream state from five minutes before. The rational and irrational swirl around one another, dancing in the darkness of the room and in the quiet of my mind.

It is the beginning of something new.

This day is like a blank page in a journal, the first note of a song, the silence of a cathedral before the people enter to pray. The expanse of each day stretches before us. For the few sleepy moments before our eyes open and our feet hit the floor, everything is possible. In these few moments, hope and terror live together.

In the darkness on the cusp of dawn, vast potential for both joy and heartbreak exists. Disappointment and awe. Discovery and failure. Today could be the day we accomplish all we want to do, or it could end in frustration over the tasks left unfinished. It could hold a defining moment that will change the trajectory of our life or be as mundane as they come. Thoughts of all the possibilities each day holds might produce excitement, fear, or an amalgamated combination of both.

So it goes with God. He is inviting us into the

concrete and the spiritual. The rational and the irrational. The known and the unknown. The darkness and the dawn. It is both hopeful and terrifying, isn't it?

My eyes open. Sleep gives way to consciousness. I unwrap myself from the covers and swing my feet over the side of the bed. The floor feels cold—but real and solid. I whisper a prayer of greeting to Him who is, as C.S. Lewis says, "not safe—but good."[1]

This is the day the Lord has made. Let us rejoice in whatever it holds.

- Does the beginning of each day produce hope, fear, or a combination of both for you?

- How content are you in times of darkness and the unknown?

- How can your present circumstances produce a deeper trust in God?

Dear Abba, You are the Lord of all my days. When I awaken each morning, You already know whether it will bring profound joy or heartbreak, if I will experience the darkness or the dawn. I am so grateful You are present in every moment, no matter what it brings. In all my circumstances, I ask for a deeper trust in You. I desire that in both abundance and need, discovery and failure, the rational and the irrational, I discover proof of Your presence and goodness. I pray that wherever I am, I am content to be there, knowing You are there too. In You, I can do all things, endure all things, and find peace in all things.

Amen.

23.

Getting the Hang of New Things

*"Jesus Christ is the same
yesterday and today and forever."*
—Hebrews 13:8

I have crossed the threshold into that part of life
when one no longer desires to jump on the
bandwagon of the latest trend. I don't jump anyway;
it hurts my knees. And trends, especially in
technology, are virtually impossible for me to keep
up with now. My son thinks it's hilarious and slightly
sad that I have no use to upgrade my phone unless
the last one accidentally landed in the toilet. My
daughter, who has developmental delays, can figure
out any app, game, or new feature on my phone

before I can figure out how to unlock it. (It makes me wonder who really has the delays in this family.)

Getting the hang of new things is not easy. It's humbling to have to learn something new that others might easily understand. Who among us likes to feel like a buffoon? But that is precisely the feeling that emerges when we take on the task of figuring out something for the first time.

When I was in my early 20s, "call waiting" was new technology. If we were on the phone (one that plugged into a wall and featured a coiled, stretchable cord that attached the base to the earpiece), it was very exciting to know we would not miss a single call. No longer would our friends hear that annoying busy signal when trying to reach us! We simply had to push the "flash" (a.k.a. hashtag) button, and it would click over to the other caller. My young, spry brain figured it out right away. For my parents, it took a bit longer.

My mom and I would be talking and all of a sudden she would say,

"Ooh, Oh! My phone beeped! What do I do? What do I do?"

I would roll my eyes and speak slowly and more than a bit condescendingly to her and tell her to click the "flash" button on her phone. She'd say, "Alright, stay on the phone. I'm going to try it." I'd hear rustling around for about 20 seconds and then,

"Hello?"

"It's still me, Mom."

"Oh. Okay, I'm going to try again. Wait there."

"Hello?"

"Still me, Mom."

"Well, I'm pushing the flash button! Why isn't this working?"

"It's not the flash button, Mom. You must be pushing something else."

"Well, I can't read all these little buttons. I think I'm pushing flash!"

"I don't know what to say, Mom. You are obviously not pushing the flash button because I'm still here."

"Ooh, there it goes again! It's beeping!"

"Try pushing another button, Mom. Maybe you'll get lucky and hit the flash."

"Hello?"

"It's still me, Mom."

My parents eventually got rid of call waiting. They decided people could call again if the line was busy. Back then, I couldn't understand why they had a hard time figuring out high-tech stuff like call waiting. Now? I get it.

Thanks to my technologically advanced kids, I actually know how to make and receive a call on my cell phone. The rest is still a mystery. They talk to me slowly and clearly (and more than a bit condescendingly) when they explain how to work my phone, the remote control, or the tablet. It makes me feel old. Mom, you've been vindicated.

We live in a fast-moving world. Technology, fashion, entertainment, and world events are constantly on the move. Our personal worlds are always morphing, too. Relationships, employment, kids, and finances never quite stay still. We regularly need to update our "emotional app" when learning how to embrace whatever "new normal" is tossed our way. It can be awkward and humbling. Can't things just slow down a bit so we can get our bearings? Then again, maybe the unsteadiness of this world is exactly what our souls need.

The demands of adjusting to a fluid life make us yearn for stability. It becomes an invitation to seek out our unchanging God. It is when we admit we can't figure things out and we need help that He speaks slowly and clearly (but never condescendingly) to our hearts. He is the assurance we long for. He is the one constant when everything else ages, changes, updates, or ceases to exist. Even though our world can adjust and shift like sand, in Him we find our feet on solid rock.

It won't be long before we are challenged again to get the hang of something new, requiring that we learn new skills, change perspective, and grow in flexibility. And asking for help requires humility and bravery. But with the confidence we have in our God—who is the same yesterday, today, and forever—we can do it, even if the kids roll their eyes at us along the way.

- How well do you adjust to the changes in your life?

- Do you have the humility to ask for help from both God and people when you need it?

- Have you been able to trust that God is a place of solid ground in this ever-changing life? Why or why not?

Dear Lord, life keeps changing. Every time I think I've finally figured out how to work something, whether it's my phone, my finances, or my relationships, I'm required to do another emotional update. It makes me long for something sure and steady. Abba, You are the solid rock on which I stand, the foundation of my life. Grant me the humility and bravery required to ask for help when I need it. Surround me with people who can show me new things. And help me to remember that in all things, You are a safe place—faithful and unchanging, constant in Your love and grace.

Amen.

24.

When the Old Bullies the New

"Whoever is a believer in Christ is a new creation.
The old way of living has disappeared.
A new way of living has come into existence."
—2 Corinthians 5:17 (GW)

I love all the potential of a new year. Like a brand-new calendar, January 1 offers an entire 12-month period of time yet to be filled up.

Every square? Blank.

The possibilities? Endless.

As the ball drops in New York and the old year comes to a close, it feels like much is made new.

God likes the New.

He loves the glory of a new morning.

He basks in the melody of a new song.

He carefully chooses a new name for each of His children.

With excitement in His voice, God invites us to witness the New He is creating before our very eyes. He likes sharing the New with us. He gets downright giddy at the thought of moving us from the Old to the New.

With Jesus Christ, all things are made new. But with new names, new mornings, and new songs, there is no place for the Old. God won't put new wine into old wineskins because the Old and the New are not compatible. The Old is unceremoniously asked to leave the party. After a few awkward protests, it leaves in a huff. And the New envelops, stirs, and moves our hearts and changes our minds. We have been transformed. The New has come.

Even so, the Old still likes to lurk in the shadows. It may not be in the building, but it is still around— peering in windows and searching for a crack in a doorway where it can come close. The Old lingers— limp and inefficient but still grasping for whatever power it might find. And the Old waits for the right time to strike.

The Old likes to get us alone.

When we have unwittingly wandered a bit outside the hub of activity and into the darker corners of the room, the Old puts its mouth right up against the crevices of our hearts and whispers. It offers dark accusations and regrets. It tries desperately to overshadow the brilliance of the New with the dull and the dead. The Old clings to ugliness, pain, and unforgiveness because that is all it has to offer. It tries to bully the New into believing it's bigger and stronger than names or songs.

And sometimes, if we are tired or hurting or not

paying attention, we listen.

But the Old holds no real power. The Old is limited to the finite time of what was. It is the New that holds the power of the unknown, untapped, and unlimited. Only the New brings fresh possibilities in a new year, new day, new hour, new moment. The Old can only replay and recycle "what has been." The Old will never breathe the air of "what is to come."

We have been made new, are being made new, and will be made new.

We are children of the God who is, who was, and who will be.

The Old has gone; the New has come.

May we live in the freedom of the New, leaving the Old far behind—just where it belongs. Whatever month it currently is, it's time to celebrate the New.

- Are there regrets that still haunt and accuse you?

- If God says that the Old has gone and the New has come, how might you be able to let go of those regrets?

- What has God made new in your life? List those things and take some time to praise Him for His goodness.

Dear Abba, I am so grateful that when I placed my life in Your hands, You made me a new creation. You took the sins and regrets of the past and separated them as far as the east is from the west. The Old has gone and the New has come. Yet sometimes the Old haunts the corners of my mind. Regrets flood back, and I am suddenly alone and ashamed once more.

When that happens, dear Abba, will You please remind me of Your truth? Will You remind me that I have been made new, and that You are still making me new? May I live in the freedom and grace of the New, leaving the Old far behind. I look forward to my future with hope, expectancy, and gratitude.

I love You.

Amen.

25.

God Creates

*"So God created mankind in his own image,
in the image of God he created them ..."*
—Genesis 1:27

"Do whatever comes to your mind! Be creative!" my friend Norma encouraged. I sat at Norma's dining room table with 15 other ladies; spread before us were about 20,000 beads, crystals, clasps, pearls, and a variety of colorful accessories to make vintage necklaces. As I looked at the dazzling amount of items to choose from, I started to get excited, thinking: *"I can do anything! I can make this necklace to be the most unique, lovely, quirky necklace anyone has ever seen! This is going to be great!"* My enthusiasm was quickly followed by a less enthusiastic thought: *"Yes, you can do anything— and it could be a disaster! You need to be careful about what beads you choose and how you use that glue gun or this entire project could be a hot mess. Besides, Norma is the one who is creative. Not you."* And with those few wayward negative thoughts, the array of jewelry supplies so beautifully displayed before me became a threat rather than an invitation. Any chance of creativity slipped through my fingers, and there I sat—frozen.

I've heard that the only difference between creative and non-creative people is that creative people simply believe they are and non-creative people believe they are not. Sitting among the beads and rhinestones, I started out in the former group, only to move to the latter with one negative thought.

Creativity requires time, open space, joy, and the freedom to explore, engage, and ignite. It requires confidence that comes from being loved and accepted for who we are. Creativity refuses to hold hands with fear and criticism. Ultimately, creativity reflects an aspect of God—the Master Creator. It's the first thing we learn about God in the Bible—He creates.

We never need to tell a child, "Be creative!" When we hand a child a few markers and a blank sheet of paper, the sky is the limit. But as we grow, often something changes. Perhaps fear has crept in. Maybe we were criticized or compared with someone else and found lacking. Maybe we were told that we are "not the artistic type." Even worse, we might have been told to "grow up" or been given the implication that creativity is for the immature. Nothing could be further from the truth.

Creation is an outpouring of who God is and how He behaves. And because we have been created in God's image, each one of us has been endowed with creativity.

This creativity will look unique and individualized as

it flows out of us. My friend Norma can take a few odd pieces of lace and pearls and make a necklace that is a work of art. For others, their creativity best shines in the way they grow a garden, cook a meal, or even formulate a spreadsheet. The freedom and joy of creativity is that it is not limited by what others believe about it. Rather, it is only limited by what we believe about ourselves.

Perhaps it has been a while since you embraced your creativity. Maybe you are not sure where to find it anymore. Maybe you didn't know you had it in the first place.

You are a reflection of a loving, merciful, gracious, creative God. His fingerprints are all over you. Discovering creative aspects about yourself is a way to learn more about the God who put them there. Value your talents and do not diminish your creativity by critical thoughts, which are not from God. You are deeply loved by Him. Trust that. May a new sense of freedom and creativity infuse your soul today.

- What voices or critical thoughts diminish your freedom to be creative?

- How does your creativity manifest itself? In scrapbooking? Cooking? Design? Teaching? Spreadsheets? Hospitality?

- List some of the creative aspects of your personality. Do you value those?

- Do you believe God values them? Why or why not?

- How does your unique creativity bless those around you?

Oh, my Creator, my life source, my foundation, and my inspiration, You are the ultimate designer! From the zebra to the duck-billed

platypus, Your fingerprints are on all of creation. Who but You could have imagined the seas and formed the mountaintops? Who but You knows how to make a tree? I rejoice and celebrate Your creation today! I celebrate not only Your creation that surrounds me, but also what You have created inside of me. I trust that, because I am made in Your image, I am meant to reflect an aspect of Your creativity. Will You show me how to embrace my unique gifts and talents? Whether my abilities are in cooking or chemistry, painting or planting, allow me to experience Your pleasure in me—and in the things I create. Guard my heart against self-condemnation or fear. Let Your love be my source of inspiration and ingenuity, that whatever passes through my hands would be glorifying to You,

my dear Abba.

Amen.

26.

In the Zone

*"We have different gifts, according
to the grace given to each of us."*
—Romans 12:6a

I've always pictured my Comfort Zone like a football field—large and rectangular, with defined lines that decree what experiences, conversations, and events are within legal play. If there is anything in my life that goes outside those perimeters, they are outside of my Comfort Zone. My game plan has been to stay within my Comfort Zone well enough to make some strong plays. If I'm feeling particularly adventurous, I'll challenge myself to travel outside the Zone long enough to get a few high fives from the crowd, have a nice 7th-inning stretch, and keep perspective of the game itself. (And yes, I'm aware I just mixed my sports metaphors. There are men groaning all over America right now. Sorry, guys. I needed to make a point.)

Lately, however, I'm coming to the conclusion that my Comfort Zone is more like a game of Kick the Can in a neighborhood cul-de-sac than an organized sports arena. There are no tidy white lines premeasured and unchanging. The edges of the Zone are loose, move around, and shape-shift depending on the play. I suspect God likes it that way. In my experience, He seems to prefer the messiness of rounded edges rather than the rigidity of square corners and measured amounts of, well, anything.

This is not to say that God is not well-defined or lacks structure. He is the solid Rock. He is unchanging and eternal and will not be shaken. But He also will not be reduced to lines, rules, and arbitrary boundaries that we humans try to set up for

Him. (If you are not sure about this point, take a look at pretty much any exchange Jesus had with the Pharisees.)

A while back, my family and I went to Ensenada, Mexico, on a missions trip. We stayed there for four days to build a small house for a family who was in desperate need of shelter. It was a noble, Christ-like thing to do. It was also an experience outside of my Comfort Zone. Really outside.

I prefer hotel rooms, white sheets, and a lot of privacy. Instead, I slept in a sleeping bag and was surrounded by about 150 other Christian brothers and sisters who seemed much more comfortable with the entire process than I. I had to wait to use the bathroom, take a shower, and eat a meal. To communicate with the locals, I made pathetic attempts to speak their language that would have made my 10th-grade Spanish teacher throw herself off a bridge in despair. And though I know how to paint, hammer nails, and measure drywall, I definitely do all of these things distinctly like a girl. In the company of extremely capable men who were working to build the house as well, I felt a bit self-conscious.

On the trip I struggled with feeling bad that I was not embracing the experience the same way a lot of other folks seemed to be. It wasn't that I was miserable or unhappy—I really did enjoy myself.

But inside of me, I didn't experience that wondrous sense of overwhelming satisfaction I expected to feel while building a home in the name of Jesus. While I appreciated what we were doing there, I was very aware that this was not "my thing."

In my desire to make myself feel worse (because feeling bad about myself is very much in my Comfort Zone), I started to think about the Apostles and how they were martyred for their faith. I imagined they had a wonderful, Christ-like attitude the whole time. I mean, heck, Peter asked to be crucified upside-down because he was not worthy to die like the Savior. And here I was, irritated that I needed to use flip-flops in the shower.

But the more I thought about Peter, the more I felt like I might be in good company with him after all. Peter was the one who wanted to know exactly the number of times he needed to forgive someone. Where are the lines? What are the rules? Jesus blew past Peter's end zone in a touchdown of grace with an answer that must have made Peter extremely uncomfortable (Matthew 18:21–35). Peter was the guy who stepped out of the boat when Jesus called to him—and for a few glorious moments, he walked on water (Matthew 14:22–33). Definitely outside his Comfort Zone. And as the Savior was being mocked and scourged, Peter was so outside of his Comfort Zone he pretended he didn't even know Jesus—and he ran off, distinctly like a girl (Mark 14:66–72). Peter did not always react well to being outside his Comfort Zone.

Some people believe that being outside your Comfort Zone is the only way God will do something amazing. Arguably, without being uncomfortable, Peter would not have learned courage or the power of trusting Jesus in circumstances that were beyond reason. He would not have experienced the incredible forgiveness that came after he denied Jesus three times.

But God works as much within our Comfort Zone as He does when He pulls us out of it.

Peter was the first one to preach to the crowds after Pentecost. Have you read that speech? Go read Acts 2:14–41. It's a humdinger. Peter was in the ZONE when he preached. Peter also wrote two books of the Bible. First Peter happens to be my favorite book in the New Testament. When he wrote that, he was in the ZONE. And God used him, blessed him, and blessed countless others because Peter flourished when he was in the Zone.

God doesn't limit Himself when it comes to His desire to grow us. He'll do amazing things within our Comfort Zone and outside of it, too.

I am much more comfortable at my computer than using a nail gun. I adore the privacy of my home versus the "group camp" experience. My inner attitude was not at all what I wish it were when I was on that missions trip; nonetheless, my Comfort Zone widened and changed from the experience of it. I discovered that it wasn't a big deal for me to use an outhouse on the job site. I didn't care that my hands were sore or my clothes were dirty. I didn't help put on the roof because I am terrified of heights, but I got pretty handy with a spackle knife. And regardless of my fluctuating comfort level, a family of six now has a roof over their heads and a place to sleep.

Some will read this as an affirmation to never, ever go on a missions trip because it's not their "thing." I get it. No judgment here.

But maybe because writing about the experience is in my Comfort Zone, others will help build a house for the poor even if they have reservations. In either Zone, God will use us if we allow Him.

See you in Mexico!

- When was the last time you did something decidedly outside your Comfort Zone?

- How has God specifically gifted you to bless others?

- What would you like to try doing, even if it is outside your Comfort Zone?

Dear Jesus, Thank You for being my solid Rock— steady and unchanging—yet so magnificent and mysterious that You will not be contained by arbitrary boundaries and notions of where You will

and will not work. Help me to discover and use what is within my Comfort Zone to bless others, to teach people about You, to be an example of kindness and compassion. But, Lord, don't leave me there. I ask You to pull me out of my Comfort Zone as well. Let my heart expand for Your people. Allow new experiences to shape and grow my understanding of You. May I be an instrument of Your peace, a defender of Your truth, and a demonstration of Your mercy both inside and outside of my Comfort Zone. And may Your name be praised and glorified as a result.

Amen.

27.

The Edges of Irises

"... You hold me by my right hand."
—Psalm 73:23

While at the Getty Museum in Los Angeles, I had the marvelous opportunity to stand in front of the breathtaking work *Irises* by Vincent van Gogh. I tried to absorb it all—the detail, the thick layers of paint, and the quick, bold strokes of color. I studied each individual part of the painting while trying to keep it in the context of the whole.

I leaned in close to the glass and would even have pressed my nose against it, but I suspected the security guards might have frowned upon that. As I studied the painting, I noticed something that any reproduction, print, or "Googled" image of this masterpiece would not show.

There are small bits of blank canvas on the edges of *Irises*. Van Gogh's easel must have held the canvas in place in these areas, so they never got covered with paint.

It's easy to miss the blank parts of *Irises*. With the way the paint leaps off the canvas, the brilliant bold pigments, and the irises themselves that seem to push past the borders of the painting, those slight blank edges don't appear to be intentional. They were simply created by what held it in place.

Van Gogh's canvas is nothing like the bright white, treated, blank canvases sold at the local Aaron Brothers or Michaels store. No, this canvas is threadbare and has a dull gray color. It's undignified. And it sits in sharp contrast to what covers 98 percent of it.

Maybe the curator working to frame this famous painting tried to cover those areas. Perhaps after some work, he decided to leave them exposed, for fear of covering up any part of the painting itself. So there they sit—the flat, dull gray patches, in the midst of bold color and depth.

Seeing this made me feel like Vincent and I shared a secret. I saw something that wasn't intended to be seen by a casual glance.

Just like the striking magnificence and detail I absorbed in Van Gogh's painting, it's the confident, picturesque beauty in other people that initially draws us to one another—the lines, the nuances, the colors that bring us further into each other's lives. Like I did with Van Gogh's *Irises*, we could study others every day and still find new things to see. There are enough layers and textures in the intricacy of others to last a lifetime of discovery. We can be the closest of friends with some people for decades and, even so, still not learn all there is to know about one another. That is the magnificence and complexity of humanity.

But it's the blank parts of the canvas that can be the most sacred parts of ourselves and others. The unfinished, the minutely exposed, and the un-intentional—those areas are rarely seen. They are the parts of our souls that may never be properly put into words. It's the dull, gray, undignified areas that we keep to ourselves and away from the casual glance. It's the vulnerable places where we, like Van Gogh's canvas, need to be held.

To discover the unfinished edges in someone else is to know that he or she is authentic—and it is a rare and beautiful gift because it creates understanding that the person hasn't been manufactured or printed, but painstakingly "created" with vulnerable places that reveal a need to be held.

This discovery is a gift for those who lean in closely, with their noses (almost) pressed against the glass and looking beyond the surface or initial glance. In the process of discovering the beauty in the threadbare parts of others, we can discover our own unfinished parts as well. As we do, we can be grateful for those who have held us—our friends, our family, and our God Himself.

Thanks, Vincent.

- Upon reflection, what are the unfinished, undignified parts of your story where you've needed to be held?

- How have you experienced being held by God and others?

- How can you go about discovering the beauty in the threadbare parts of others?

Dear Abba, there are parts of my life and my

personality that are strong, vibrant, and easily seen and known by all. Thank You for the beauty in the way You created me. Thank You for the bright colors and the deep hues that make up my life. There are threadbare parts of my own soul that need to be seen as well. They are rarely noticed by others, and sometimes I keep them hidden from view altogether. Even so, You always see all of me, the bold flowers and the unfinished edges alike. Thank You for Your steadfast love and Your gaze that never wavers and never looks away. Oh, God, thank You for holding me in the places I need it most. And I pray that as others reveal their threadbare parts to me, I will be a trustworthy caretaker of their vulnerabilities as You are for me.

Amen.

28.

Remembering to Float

"When you pass through the waters, I will be with you; and when you pass through the rivers, they will not sweep over you."
—Isaiah 43:2

Growing up in Southern California, I often went to the beach in the summer. My siblings, friends, and I boogie-boarded, dug holes to China in the sand, and built elaborate sand castles with deep moats. We jumped the waves, dug our feet into the sand, and tried to stand while the waves worked to knock us over. We caught sand crabs and laughed as we put those poor, defenseless creatures in buckets and let them swim around and hopelessly dig into the bright orange plastic in a futile attempt to escape.

(Sand crabs are the pill bugs of the ocean. I am not sure what ecological importance they have—if any— but they provide *hours* of entertainment for kids at the beach.)

Back then, before I cared about keeping my hair nice or how I looked in my bathing suit, I liked to play in the ocean.

I would dip under the waves—swimming past where they broke along the shoreline. I still remember the feeling; the more submerged I was, the more the sounds above the water were muffled and faint. Even with my eyes squeezed shut, I could tell that it was much darker underneath as the light of the sun slipped away. I could feel the heaviness of the ocean water pressing against my ears and the pressure of the air held in my lungs. Under water, there was a distinct rhythm to the way the ocean moved. While the waves were not seen, their motion could be felt.

A few times, I would surface just as another wave

was moving toward me. I only had time for a quick and shallow gasp of air before I would be under water again. That always made me panic a bit, because I didn't have time to grab a full breath of air and there I would be, avoiding the wave, under the water, with very little breath to spare. I would be afraid my lungs were going to explode or I wouldn't be able to come up in time and would end up drowning right there in the ocean while my friends were still imprisoning sand crabs.

Then there was the time I went out farther than usual. A huge wave (at least it was huge in my 9-year-old brain) washed over me. I had just enough time to take in a bit of air before I was knocked over so hard that my head went under my feet. Because I couldn't reach the sandy bottom, I couldn't tell which way was up and where to swim to the surface. My eyes were closed, and the shore was too far away to hear even muffled sounds. I was wholly disoriented and completely terrified.

I remember instinctively reaching out my hands for something, anything, to grab on to, but there was nothing but more water.

Just before absolute panic took over, I remembered the first thing a person is taught when learning to swim—before the breaststroke, before the freestyle, before even learning how to breathe in rhythm.

I remembered how to float.

As hard as it was, I fought against my panic and allowed my body to simply go limp. Without any sense of direction and with very little air remaining, I floated to the top of the water. By then, the wave had passed. I found the surface of the water, gasped for oxygen, and felt a surge of relief. Tired, scared, and relieved, I found the strength to swim back to shore.

Everyone on the sand was exactly where I had last seen them. My mom was still reading her Danielle

Steele novel between nagging the kids not to get sand on the blanket. My brother was still grabbing handfuls of Cheetos without wiping the sand from his hands, and the kids around us were still digging holes and dumping sand crabs into buckets. The whole experience happened so quickly that no one even noticed. I dried off, grabbed a few sandy Cheetos, and helped dig a hole to China.

In our grown-up world, when life knocks our feet out from under us and we can't tell which way is up anymore, it is a perfectly natural reaction to fight against what feels like certain death. Like I did under water, we reach out and grasp for something, anything, to steady us. When we can no longer tell which way is up, our arms flail, our legs kick, and panic rises. Our lungs tighten, and our chest gets heavy.

But we who trust in the name of the Lord will not drown. The waves will not destroy us. In times of distress, let us remember to float.

God has equipped you for this life and its difficult and devastating times. With Him, you can withstand the waves that crash over your head and make you lose your footing. He's designed you to float—but floating requires you let go. It will conflict with every instinct that wants to take over and continue to fight. Let go anyway. He's got you. This wave is not a surprise to Him. Trust Him as your Creator, your Defender, your Friend. He is with you in these deep waters, and this wave will not sweep over you and carry you away. Instead, you will float in His care, in His attention, and in His saving grace.

- In what ways have the waves of life threatened to pull you under?

- How deeply do you trust that God will not let the waves sweep over you?

- What does it feel like to let go and "float" in the midst of fear?

Dear Abba, I praise You for Your faithfulness to me. You prevent the waves from pulling me under completely. You are the God of the wind and waves, and You know the storms that will come my way. When I get panicked, when I am afraid, will You help me remember to float? In Your arms, I am safe to let go. With You, my legs and arms no longer need to reach out in desperation for something, anything, to hold on to. You, my Savior, already have me. Remind me that You are holding me. As my faith deepens, may I more quickly remember to float, that I will find the safety and care of Your love even sooner. Thank You for Your steadfast protection.

Amen.

29.

I Am

"God said to Moses, 'I am who I am.' "
—Exodus 3:14

I am.

God's Word tells me who I am.

I am because You are.

Because You are God.

You are the Alpha

You are the Omega

The beginning

The end

And all that lies in between.

You are "I AM."

You are.

I am.

I am, because You are.

I am accepted

I am Your child

I am Your friend

I belong to You.

I have been bought with a price

I am a member of Christ's Body

I am united with You.

I am justified

I am redeemed

I am forgiven

I am complete

I am blessed

I am chosen.

I am because You are.

You are my Savior

My shepherd

My provider

My peace

My righteousness.

You are Jehovah

El-Roi

El-Shaddai

Yahweh

Shalom.

You are, so I am.

I am hidden with Christ

I am born of God and the evil one cannot touch me

I cannot be separated from the love of God

I am sealed with the promise of the Holy Spirit.

I am Your workmanship

I am Your temple

I am a citizen of heaven

I am Yours, set apart for good works.

I am. You ARE.

You are the Lord God Almighty

The Lord Jesus Christ

Lord of All

Lord of Glory

Lord of Hosts

Lord of Lords

King of Kings

My King and my Lord.

I am because You are

my, our, the

I AM.

30.

Letting Go of Feeling Bad

*"Therefore, there is now no condemnation
for those who are in Christ Jesus."*
—Romans 8:1

I like to set goals and dream big. I like to take on projects and strive to be better than I am. I always want to be learning, growing, and developing. I suspect you do, too. Goals are an important part of personal growth and maturity, and part of setting goals involves reflecting on past experiences.

How did the last goal work out?

What was learned?

What can be done differently the next time?

When I assess my past plans and goals, I reflect on the things I accomplished and the things I didn't. Of course I feel great about my successes. I feel motivated and have a sense of contentment about what I've done well. But the things I've failed at, forgotten, or left unfinished?

I feel bad.

Most of us realize we will not succeed at everything. We're only human. Setting big goals, making big plans, and wanting more for ourselves are exhilarating and inspiring. But when we have fallen short, we're sometimes not quite ready to shrug our shoulders and move on. We want to do something about it. We want to take control of or find reasons for our failings. Perhaps we want to make sure that our brain knows that our heart knows we've failed.

Given the chance to try again, we *want* to do better. We *try* to do better. We *work* to do better. There's nothing wrong with hard work and second chances.

But sometimes we cross the line into thinking that feeling bad about our present failures will ensure future success.

Have you ever failed at a diet plan? I have. And I'm really good at feeling bad about it.

It's true, not fitting into a pair of jeans feels bad. But feeling bad about not fitting into those jeans? That is another issue entirely. Ruminating about the ways you've failed at your diet goals or how much of a loser you are will never bring positive results. Feeling bad doesn't burn calories. It only invites shame. And shame invites isolation. And isolation invites eating ice cream. And the cycle continues. I'm fairly certain no one ever found the motivation to climb Mount Everest by feeling bad.

Acknowledging an unmet goal is healthy and mature. Understanding that it might be necessary to adjust a plan of action is crucial. But feeling bad is not fruitful and, even more, not godly.

Brennan Manning writes, *"In order to be free to be faithful to [Jesus], to others and ourselves, we must be liberated from the damnable imprisonment of self-hatred, freed from the shackles of projectionism, perfectionism, moralism/legalism, and unhealthy guilt. Freedom for fidelity demands freedom from enslavement."*[1]

Let's set big goals. Go for it. Make resolutions. Dream big. And when some of those dreams don't work out? We will reassess and recalibrate. But we must refuse to be shackled by the prison of feeling bad. For all the times we will fail, fall short, and remain unfinished, we will also remain loved by our God, who is infinitely pleased with us. And that feels so very good.

- Do you ever try to motivate yourself by feeling bad? How does that work out for you?

- How does taking responsibility for a failure differ from simply "feeling bad"?

- What goals and dreams do you have?

- Are you allowing past failures to stand in the way of future success?

Dear Jesus, I want so much to do great things and accomplish great things. I want to continue to grow, develop, and mature in You. I don't want to be shackled by past regrets. I don't want my failures to prevent me from taking big leaps of faith for You. If there are areas of sin in my life that I ignore or hide, will You show those to me? And when they are revealed, I pray that instead of simply "feeling bad," I would offer my brokenness to You—asking for forgiveness and allowing You to refine my heart and shape my mind. I pray that my life is one of successes, failures, mountaintops, and valleys, too,

because all of those reflect an abundant life of

faithful living. My desire is to live in Your freedom

and grace. I choose this day to let go of feeling bad.

I will trust that no matter how often I miss the mark,

I am not condemned, not because of anything

I can do or accomplish, but because

You alone are my Savior, Redeemer, and King.

Amen.

31.

On Robin Williams and the Love of God

*"If I say, 'Surely the darkness will hide me
and the light become night around me,' even
the darkness will not be dark to you; the night will
shine like the day, for darkness is as light to you."*
—Psalm 139:11–12

The suicide of Robin Williams has been heavy on my mind. In the past, when someone died, there would be a "wake"—a time when friends and family gathered together to mourn. What a perfect description. When people die, even when expected, it's like the person took off at a high rate of speed, and the rest of us are left experiencing the wake—

the aftermath of that departure—in an ocean of unanswered questions. Waves of grief and torrents of anger, sadness, and desperation roll over us and swirl around us, and it feels like we are going under. In the case of suicide, we are slapped hard across the face and left to dog-paddle in waters far too deep and dark to think we could possibly make sense of such a cruel, bullying departure.

"Didn't he know that Jesus loved him?" was a question I saw posted on a Facebook feed. It felt like a punch in the gut. "WHO CARES??" I impulsively wanted to cyber-shout back. Children lost their father, a wife lost her husband, countless friends and others are choking on the brutality of the death of someone they loved. At the moment when Mr. Williams took that belt and looped it around his neck, whether or not Jesus loved him was inconsequential in his tortured mind.

It's a difficult thing—this love of Jesus. On one hand, we are taught that the love of God makes all the difference in our lives. To understand and accept the love of Jesus is the single most important thing a person can do to ensure not only a future life in heaven, but also a life of abundance and meaning in the present. Yet, on the other hand, the love of God does not remove heartbreak, death, depression, or the violence of the mind or of this world from our lives. There are people who love Jesus, yet they still get cancer. They still get divorced. Their children die. They are angry, overwhelmed, afraid, and left dog-paddling in the wake of the loss and pain of living.

"Didn't he know that Jesus loved him?"

I don't know if Robin Williams did or not. I have always resented this type of bumper sticker mentality that somehow if a person knows that Jesus loves them, all will be well. Sometimes, that is the case. But sometimes it's definitely not.

"Come with me" was the invitation Jesus gave.

Many responded—and still do. But what has penetrated my mind and heart and rooted my relationship with Christ is the reverse—that He, in fact, will come with me.

And I know where I go.

Jesus will be with me in the muck and mire of my pettiness, my jealousy, my short temper, and my malicious thoughts. He will walk with me into the darkness of depression and in those moments, days, and weeks of despair that envelop me and pull me into dark, terrifying waters. He will look headlong into my faithlessness, my weakness, my fear, and my sin and will not blink. He will hold my hand even when I don't want to hold His.

Jesus' arms held lepers and touched their filthy, disease-infested bodies. His hands were soiled with sickness and blood. His feet were caked with dirt and debris, and those same feet were washed with a prostitute's hair and tears. He sweat blood and anguished in the Garden; He called out to His friends and His God—and in His dying moments on that cross, He got no response from either.

Recently I have spent some time ruminating on a quote from the movie *The Shawshank Redemption*: *"[He] crawled to freedom through five hundred yards of shit smelling foulness I can't even imagine, or maybe I just don't want to. Five hundred yards ... that's the length of five football fields, just shy of half a mile."*[1]

Indeed, Jesus did this for us.

In the darkness of depression and hopelessness, in the midst of sorrow, grief, unanswered questions, and the sheer vulnerability of living this life, we crawl our own football fields of filth.

And Jesus is there too.

Is that love? You bet it is. It's the kind of love that has made all the difference in my life. There is not a place I travel in my mind and heart that Jesus did not go first. He knew exactly what He was getting with me and decided to take up residence anyway.

Love can be beautiful, winsome, comforting, kind, and gracious. It is the inspiration of Hallmark cards, bumper stickers, and simple children's songs. Though I am blessed by those things, it's not the "nice" side of Jesus' love that has transformed my life. It's the grittiness. It's the fierceness. The love that got dirt under His fingernails has kept hope running through my wearied veins.

Didn't Mr. Williams know Jesus loved him? I truly hope he did. And while that knowledge might not have prevented him from taking his life in the midst of his torment, it might have brought him some measure of comfort. Because in our worst moments—when darkness reigns and we are pulled under into the waters of death—Jesus is still there. His forehead sweaty, His side bloodied, His feet scarred. With His calloused, muddied hands He holds onto us when our grip slips, and He crawls with us through the length of five football fields to guide us to freedom.

Jesus has invited me to come with Him. I've accepted. Incredibly, He has the grittiness and ferocity to come with me.

My prayer is that in those final moments of his life, in the midst of unspeakable desperation and darkness, Mr. Williams came face-to-face with a God who was right there with him. A God who looked headlong into his heartbreaking decision and didn't blink. And in that moment, I hope Mr. Williams knew he was loved.

- Have you been blindsided by the death of a loved one? Have you been able to find comfort in the love of God, or do you struggle with bringing your grief to Him?

- What does it feel like to think that Jesus goes with you everywhere—even to the darkest parts of your thoughts and actions? Is it uncomfortable or a relief?

- Can you intentionally invite Jesus into the darkest parts of your life, with the understanding that He knew exactly what He was getting into when He took up residence in your heart?

Oh my Abba, my Father, my Savior, my Redeemer— my heart aches at the horror of death and the grief it causes us. Thank You, Jesus, that Your death on the cross made it so that death has lost its sting and we can step into eternity with You. Today, I pray for those who are mourning. I pray for the families and friends affected by the suicide of someone they loved.[2] I pray for those who are so alone they can't find their way out of the darkness of their

circumstances. I pray for Your presence to envelop and enlighten them and to offer them the hope that shines into those long football fields of desolation. Oh Lord, I am humbled and grateful that no matter where I go, no matter my thoughts, my actions, my circumstances or standing, You are with me, going before me, standing beside me, protecting my back. In my darkest moments of despair, may I reach out and find You there—gripping my hand and reminding me that I am never, not for one moment, alone in this world.

Amen.

32.

Gathering Dandelions

*"But God chose the foolish things of the world
to shame the wise; God chose the weak things
of the world to shame the strong."*
—1 Corinthians 1:27

My first real boyfriend entered my life when I was 16.
His name was David. He had great eyes and a great
smile, and he was smart and kind. Even better? He
had a car. It was a two-door coupe with bucket seats,
and it was painted my favorite color. It weaved in
and out of traffic easily because it was small and fast.
It had a stereo that cranked up Bruce Springsteen
and a hatchback trunk that was just perfect to hold
school backpacks. It was dreamy and cool, and I
loved it.

David's yellow Ford Pinto was perfect.

Wait ... what's that chuckle about? Doesn't every red-blooded American woman dream of the day her Prince Charming would show up to sweep her off her feet and carry her off in a bright yellow Pinto?

Maybe not.

But to my 16-year-old heart, that Pinto might as well have been a Ferrari. It was magical.

I'm more sophisticated now. I like leg room, seat warmers, and dual air bags. I get my hair cut at a salon where they don't charge separately for a shampoo. I like restaurants with waiters, hotels with pillow top beds, and shoes made of genuine soft leather. I like my coffee made with freshly ground beans. I wonder if David does, too.

When I was about 7 years old I decided to bring my elderly neighbor a bouquet of flowers. I wanted to share the beauty in my front yard. I gathered up all the dandelions I could find and nervously knocked on the door. When she opened it, I presented her with my riches. She took them, smiled, and said, "Oh! Dandelions! Thank you!" I smiled back. Then she said, "Did you know that dandelions are actually weeds? But thank you anyway, sweetie." I nodded and walked away. Some of the magic did too. I don't think I made dandelion bouquets after that.

Why is it that we allow other people to decide what is beautiful, valuable, or sophisticated? Who decided a dandelion is a weed and not a flower anyway? (There is probably some scientific explanation for it, but why should that make a difference?)

At 16, I thought that yellow Pinto was the best car ever. Would I give up my seat warmers and leg room for one now? Likely not. But the Ford Pinto will always be a great car in my eyes.

No one has the right to decide what is beautiful to your heart. Just because something is a weed or a crappy car in one person's eyes doesn't mean it needs to be in yours.

Jesus is masterful at seeing the exquisite in odd places, such as in the eyes of a tax collector, the alabaster jar of a sinful woman, and the dying words of a thief on a cross. He came for both the sophisticated and the rubes. Jesus finds beauty in those who have been mistaken for weeds. He loves the unlovely and sees each one of us in amazing, unimaginably beautiful ways. It's magical.

I've dealt with depression most of my life. For a lot of that time, I tried really, really hard to pluck it out, like a weed in a garden. I was convinced it didn't belong, that it took away from whom I'm meant to be. I was embarrassed and ashamed of this fractured, weak area of myself. I asked God, over and over again, to remove it.

So far, He hasn't.

But if I believe He is a good God (and I do) and that He loves me (and I do), then I am led to believe He has left it there for a reason.

Struggling with depression has taught me over and over again to turn to God for strength, for peace, for courage. It has kept me in utter dependence upon my Abba. In that way, it has been a gift. I don't ever want to be well enough, competent enough, or strong enough to lose sight of how much I need Him. This gift of weakness keeps me focused on Jesus. For that, I'm grateful.

I no longer feel ashamed of the depression that still comes and goes like the tide. I'm beginning to understand that if God is comfortable with it remaining, then perhaps I can get comfortable with it, too. I've mistaken my deepest struggles for weeds, when they just might be the most beautiful parts of my life.

Today, let's find beauty in odd places. Let's gather

bouquets of dandelions and take a drive along the coast in a yellow Ford Pinto and see all of the lovely, unsophisticated, unexpected things that can bring us wholeness and joy. What a magical, beautiful day it will be!

- What do you find secretly and oddly beautiful—even if others might think it weird?

- Are there activities, hobbies, or items that used to bring you joy, but now have been forgotten or abandoned because they seemed silly or unsophisticated?

- What aspects of your personality, struggles, and experiences have you or others mistaken for a weed? How does God find those same things beautiful?

Dear Abba, You have a funny way of looking at things. My perspective on beauty doesn't always match Yours. On occasion, I let the world divert my attention from what is beautiful to what is bright. I often see situations in my life and I am sure they are weeds, better plucked out than gathered and celebrated. Yet You have ordained them, allowed them, and chosen to leave them where they are. Help me, like You, to find what is lovely in these odd places. Let me see the beauty in the pain and struggles I've mistaken for weeds. Allow me to celebrate the simple and embrace the unsophisticated in my own life and in the lives of others, that my thoughts and actions will become more reflective of You. You bring beauty to what most take for a weed. I love that about You, Abba.

Amen.

33.

~~Jumping~~ Falling from Trees

"Be alert, be present. I'm about to do something brand-new. It's bursting out! Don't you see it?"
—Isaiah 43:18 (MSG)

When I was a little girl, I got stuck in a tree.

I remember being terrified to jump down, knowing that I would surely break my arm or leg. More likely, I would die. (I was prone to drama back then. I'm much better now. Okay, not really. Just ask my husband … or my kids … or anyone who knows me.)

My dad called me to jump down into his arms. While I bear-hugged the branch with both arms and legs, lying facedown into the musty-smelling wood, my father stood below with arms open, feet securely planted, a look on his face of patient love. "Come on, Melissa," he said. "I promise I will catch you." I looked at his outstretched arms with suspicion and wondered if he was being overly confident.

"One ... two ... THREE!" my father counted enthusiastically.

I didn't budge.

It's not that my father had a history of dropping me. As a matter of fact, there isn't one instance that comes to mind where he did. Yet his arms looked so far away, and the tree felt large and strong beneath me. It was difficult to imagine voluntarily unwrapping myself from the security of what I knew to fall into empty space before landing (maybe) in my father's arms.

And it would certainly be *falling*—which is not the same as jumping. I was in no position to get my feet underneath me to make a decisive, courageous leap.

Getting out of that tree would require that I let go.

Sometimes in the experiences of life we get the opportunity to incrementally climb one branch after the other, higher and higher. It happens so quietly and slowly, we don't even notice how far we've come. There are relationships, jobs, ministries, and goals that make us flourish. These experiences are beautiful, good, and true. They give us the opportunity to discover our gifting, passions, and abilities. Even when the journey gets harrowing, it makes us stronger. The climb allows us to sit in the treetops, enjoy the view, and breathe in the warm air of confidence and the cool breezes of God's grace.

After a while, we get comfortable. The view is familiar, the branches are sure, and we've been safe and loved where we are. We come to know what to expect, and we like it.

Then, we hear Abba's voice—and He tells us He has something new in store. He invites us to make a change, to leave the familiar. When we hear Abba's quiet nudging to jump (fall) into His arms and start a new adventure, it's hard to let go of what we know and love. At the mere thought of it, we might clutch tighter to what we can touch, feel, and grasp.

But Abba's gentle, steady voice continues to call. He stands below with an upturned face, outstretched arms, and feet solidly planted on the ground, assuring us His arms are strong enough.

When God asks us to step out in faith, to let go of the familiar and head in a new direction, it would be fantastic if we were to rise to our feet and jump into His invitation with aplomb. But most of the time we will not have that confidence. We will weigh the odds. We will tell ourselves, God, and anyone else who will listen why this leap of faith makes no sense whatsoever. We will wonder if the vision in our mind is from God or the result of last night's sushi. If it's His call, though, He will continue to call.

Our Father does not have a history of dropping us. So when His sweet voice invites us to something new, one by one our fingers can loosen their grip on the safe and comfortable.

One … two … three … ~~JUMP!~~ (FALL!)

As the wind rushes in your ears and the treetops get smaller and smaller, you can look up at all the ways you've been blessed by where you've been. Your heart can cry out in gratitude for all that was, and it can open itself up to all that is unknown.

When Abba calls, we can trust His voice and His timing. We can take big chances. We can make way for new adventures. We may not do it gracefully. It might be more of a "trust fall" than a leap of faith, but that doesn't really matter. Either way, our Father has promised to catch us. And He will.

- How do you respond to God's call? Are you a "leaper" or a "faller"?

- Consider the things that are most familiar, most safe, and most reliable in your life. Are they there because they continue to bring blessings and growth, or have you been clutching onto the familiar rather than heeding God's calling?

- Are there nudgings you've been getting to follow God on a new adventure? What are they, and how can you begin to jump (or fall) into His arms and trust Him to catch you?

Dear Abba, there are parts of my journey that have brought me so much joy, growth, and comfort. They have allowed me to flourish. I have felt Your hand

upon me in those circumstances, and I've discovered my gifting, my talents, and more about how You have shaped me. I hope I have served You well in them. Thank You so much for the amazingly good things in my life. If there are circumstances or relationships or work that I need to let go of because You now desire me to go somewhere new, will You reveal that to me? If I get scared and grasp tighter because I want to feel safe, will You be faithful to continue to call my name and invite me to jump (or more likely, fall) into Your arms? I want to be open to what You are asking me to grasp as much as what You want me to release. Most of all,

I want to live an obedient life, one that goes to high places of vision and victory yet is willing to let go of the familiar and safe to follow You. Thanks for waiting patiently beneath the tree with outstretched arms and a voice of compassion and grace.

I know You will catch me. You always have.

You always will.

Amen.

34.

Surrounded

"Therefore, since we are surrounded by such a huge crowd of witnesses to the life of faith, let us strip off every weight that slows us down, especially the sin that so easily trips us up. And let us run with endurance the race God has set before us."
—Hebrews 12:1 (NLT)

This verse makes me uncomfortable. *A "huge crowd of witnesses" is surrounding me while I run this race?* I think to myself. This race, on most days, feels more like a crawl or a meander than an Olympic event. And furthermore, I really don't want God's saints watching me and my sweaty body crawl awkwardly by. Can't I just keep this race between me and God?

And then I think, *Who exactly is watching?* Mother

Teresa can't possibly be impressed. After all, I complain if my Keurig goes on the fritz. Martin Luther probably watches through his fingers with one eye open. My race-running might be too scary to take it all in at once.

I stumble, fall down, twist my ankle, stroll, and sometimes run this race. My speed and strength are not terribly consistent, but I'm moving. Still, it's a bit intimidating to think St. Francis of Assisi saw the time when I flushed the goldfish I forgot to feed. I am embarrassed to think that the same people who have given their very lives for the cause of Christ are witnesses to my shallow doubts and fears.

If we are Christ-followers, Scripture refers to us as saints. I don't feel like one. But I doubt Mother Teresa felt like one either. After she died, it was revealed that she had a "50-year crisis of faith." She wrote, *"I am told God loves me—and yet the reality of darkness and coldness and emptiness is so great that nothing touches my soul."*[1]

Perhaps Mother Teresa and I have more in common than anyone would think. Maybe we all do.

We are surrounded by a great cloud of witnesses. Saints such as Francis of Assisi, who lived his early life carousing and enjoying wine, women, and song. And Martin Luther, who started the Protestant Reformation but at the same time was plagued with crippling depression. Author Brennan Manning wrote, *"Define yourself radically as one beloved by God. This is the true self. Every other identity is illusion."*[2] Mr. Manning died several years ago; he never beat his alcoholism. The apostle Peter, forgiven by Jesus after his night of denial and charged with building God's Church, still wimped out and ditched the Gentiles at the first whiff of peer pressure. Paul most likely experienced depression. David? Adulterer. Thomas? Don't get me started.

We are surrounded by a great crowd of witnesses, it is true. We are encircled by the saints of heaven who lurched, tripped, and fell but dusted themselves off and kept going ... and who ran their race. They lean forward with great intensity, whispering in our ears and shouting from the rooftops, "Onward! Onward!"

They have finished the race. But since Jesus still had His scars after the resurrection, I suspect the saints do, too. Battle wounds that have healed yet remain as a testament to the One who came to not *"call the righteous, but sinners"* (Mark 2:17).

Shall we run this race together, you and I? I will ignore the toilet paper stuck to your shoe if you ignore my sweaty armpits. Let's just keep going. We have a lot of people cheering us on.

- How are you feeling these days? Are the roads currently level in your race, or does it feel like an upward climb?

- What do you feel when you consider that you are surrounded by witnesses?

- How might your faith as well as your frailty be a source of encouragement to others on the journey?

Dear Abba, thank You for the great cloud of witnesses who have gone before me. Thank You that they are people who fell down, got up, and kept going. Thank You for their example of both faith and frailty. Thank You for calling me a "saint" when I feel anything but saintly. In my own race, I pray that I can serve as a witness and an encouragement to those surrounding me here in this life. I ask for Your strength, Your endurance, and Your blessing as I go onward, forward, ever toward You, my Savior, my Source, and my Salvation.

Amen.

35.

The Things I Never Got

"Now faith is confidence in what we hope for and assurance about what we do not see."
—Hebrews 11:1

I was 10 years old when I answered the door to a man holding an accordion. He had a wide smile and called me "young lady" in a way that made me feel slightly giddy*. The gentleman asked if he might have a few minutes of our time to introduce me to the wonderful world of the accordion.

He guaranteed he would teach me to play a song in under 10 minutes. With visions of a musical career stretching out before me, I begged my dad to give him a chance. My father begrudgingly agreed. So there in my family's living room, true to his word, the traveling accordion pitchman taught me to play a simple song.

I saw my life's calling that night; I would be the world's foremost accordion player. I'd travel the globe with my band, and everyone would know my name. The man offered lessons for the amazing price of $199. I threw myself on my dad's mercy and begged and pleaded. I wanted those accordion lessons more than I'd ever wanted anything else. My father wasn't as enthusiastic. Up against the slick smile of a salesman and the pleading eyes of his daughter, my dad stood strong. The answer was no.

I was devastated. I've never picked up the accordion again.

All these years later, I have no desire to play the accordion**. My heart moved on from this. Still, there are other things I've wanted and not gotten.

If we believe that our life is in God's hands, that He wants the best for us, that the things He says "no" to are part of His plan to prosper and not harm us, then it should be easy to let go of the things we've wanted and not received, right?

[Insert uncomfortable silence here.]

In the truth of my embarrassingly capricious heart, what "should be" doesn't always line up with what is. Sometimes it's downright painful to let go of the things we desire, especially when hope—fascinating, frustrating, and firm—remains.

Hope considers that God's "no" might actually be a "not yet." Perhaps He has bigger and better plans; maybe He's preparing something for us we cannot yet imagine. Only it's difficult to hope in something we cannot imagine. Our brain naturally defaults to the things our eyes can see. The things we find attractive. The things we want. And the belief that God has our best life in mind when He says "no" easily gives way to what is sitting in front of us on a shelf, in a car lot, or across the garden. (See Genesis 3.) Our hope loses focus.

Hebrews 11:1 says, *"Now faith is confidence in what we hope for and assurance about what we do not see."* Apparently, that which we have confidence in makes all the difference between focused hope and misplaced desire.

Focused hope allows us to see the God who has manifested Himself all around us. It allows us to see His magnificence in the ocean, the eyes of our kids, and the beauty of friendships. It offers us abundant possibility in the scarcest of options.

Focused hope gives our restless souls a place to linger, a place to exhale.

We cannot see the future He has planned, and we're not going to be able to control most of it anyway. We've only been assured that at our last breath, we will be with Him.

In my humanity, my heart breaks a little when I don't get what I really, really want. But faith allows us to have confident hope that the One who says "no" loves us beyond measure. Our hope has focus when directed to His proven lovingkindness. And when we press into God through faith, heartbreak gives way to contentment in the things we do not understand.

So what to do with our "unfocused" hope? Where do I go with the next accordion lesson that is possibly a desire of my heart but easily could be just the next shiny thing to catch my attention? I can try to handle it myself—but that never turns out well. (Revisit Genesis 3.)

Instead, we bring it to Him. All of it. We offer Him the vulnerability of asking for what we want. We throw ourselves on His mercy and beg and plead. I'm often embarrassed by the frivolity that captures my desires. I'm rarely begging for world peace. Of late, I really, really, really want an RV. Really, really. But part of hope is bringing our raw confessions to our Father. And intimate faith is leaning our heads against His chest and bawling our eyes out as we move toward acceptance when His answer is "no."

When we come to our Father with this kind of faith and hope, He proves trustworthy every time. And whatever His answer to our begging and pleading, He can be praised equally for all the blessings He's given and all the things we never receive.

- What do you really, really long for?

- What do you imagine about God when He says "no" to you?

- Are you willing to go to God with your deepest desires, no matter how frivolous or embarrassing, how vulnerable it is to ask? Why or why not?

Dear Father, my heart longs for so many things. Some are frivolous; some feel like I might die if I don't get them. Only You know the true difference between the two. Only You know where the desires of my heart and Your will intersect. Oh, God, how my heart aches for the things I've desired yet not received. Remind me of Your faithfulness in every circumstance. May I rejoice and be grateful when You lavish me with good gifts. And when Your answer is "no," may I draw near to You, my Abba, to rest my head on Your chest and bawl my eyes out, trusting Your goodness in all the things You give and all the things I've never received.

Amen.

*I'm still giddy if someone calls me "young lady."

**My husband says I should thank my dad profusely. He indicated that a red-headed accordion player might not be the apex of social acceptance. He might have a point.

36.

The KNOW-Know

"For we do not have a high priest who is unable to empathize with our weaknesses, but we have One who has been tempted in every way, just as we are— yet He did not sin. Let us then approach God's throne of grace with confidence, so that we may receive mercy and find grace to help us in our time of need."
—Hebrews 4:15–16

Every Christmas season, I feel a renewed sense of joy that I don't work in any retail business. Years ago, I was the assistant manager for a clothing store. I refolded the same sweaters more times than Mel Tormé has crooned "Have Yourself a Merry Little Christmas." I worked 10–12 hours a day and developed recurring blisters from standing in heels for so long. My back and body ached, and I barely saw my husband. Some customers were very nice, but most were oblivious to the mess they were making. Some people were downright nasty.

Since then, I've never looked at Christmas shopping in the same way. Now I go out of my way to be particularly kind to retail employees. I refold things. I don't leave stuff in the dressing room. I get off the phone when I am paying for my items.

I've walked a mile in the high heels of retail employees. And I'm different because of it. Previously, I knew it was tough on them at Christmastime. But after my experience being one of them, I KNOW-know.

When Jesus Christ was born, God Himself walked in our shoes. Jesus, fully human, had days when His feet hurt, His back ached and He got blisters. People pushed and shoved around Him. Some were kind. Some were oblivious. Some were downright nasty.

Through Jesus, God KNOW-knows what it's like to be lonely, wearied, or betrayed by loved ones. He knows what it's like to hurt, be disappointed, have questions, grieve, and experience regret. He understands the feeling of being exhausted. He knows what it's like to be tempted. The One who knows where every star in the night sky is located also knows what it's like to stub a toe, smash a finger, or sneeze from a cold. He's been hungry and felt thirst. Because of Jesus, God KNOW-knows what it is like to walk around in our shoes. Furthermore, not only does He understand the experiences common to all humanity, He also KNOW-knows you—your habits, your hopes, your frustrations, and your longings.

Jesus left the majesty of the heavens to experience mundane, messy humanity. Why? He did it so that the next time you ask, "Do you know what I am going through, God?" He can answer, "Yes, my child. I do. I KNOW-know. I am here with you, and I will never leave you. I KNOW-know you, and I deeply love you."

Today, may we come to a deeper understanding of how God intimately knows and loves each of us. May this understanding cause us to live in more joy, peace, freedom, and grace in *every* season of our lives.

- What are the feelings and experiences in your life that you most long for others to understand about you?

- How well do you feel understood and known by God?

- Imagine what it was like for Jesus, the Son of God, to walk around on this earth. As flesh and blood, what did Jesus need to endure?

- What did He get to enjoy as a result of His physical presence on earth?

- How might these common human experiences draw you closer to Him?

Dear Jesus, You love me so much and You want to connect with me so deeply that You became a human being. You had all the glories of heaven at Your fingertips, yet You chose being human—to stub Your toe, to get sick, and also to experience the comfort of a hug and the joy of a hot meal at the end of the day. You are so holy and glorious that nothing is outside of Your control, yet in Your humility and grace, You set it all aside to find me, to connect with me, to KNOW-know me. I am overwhelmed at Your kindness. Thank You, Jesus, for coming down, reaching out, and walking a mile and more in my shoes. May I live out of the deep understanding that there is no place I will travel and

nothing I will endure that You have not experienced first. You KNOW-know me. You are a God of compassion and comfort, and I will praise You all the days of my life.

Amen.

37.

Staring Down Fear

*"For I am convinced that neither death nor life,
neither angels nor demons, neither the present nor
the future, nor any powers, neither height nor depth,
nor anything else in all creation, will be able to
separate us from the love of God that is in
Christ Jesus our Lord."*
—Romans 8:38–39

I don't like fear. But fear seems to like me. Fear comes to visit regularly. It's not like I invite fear. I don't skydive, wrestle sharks, or eat strange foods. I like seatbelts, helmets, and knowing that my airplane seat cushion can be used as a flotation device. Yet fear commonly barges its way into my heart without so much as a polite knock.

How do we deal with such a rude, uninvited guest as fear? In Scripture, we are told over and over, "Don't be afraid," yet simply trying to not be afraid doesn't work very well. It's kind of like telling you to stop thinking of a pink elephant on a bicycle. It can hardly be helped. Ignoring fear only emboldens it. Hiding it helps it grow—like mold in a dark, damp corner.

The best course of action is to look fear squarely in the face and describe to God what we see. When we admit our fears to the Lord, an interesting thing happens: Courage shows up. It's a deep, abiding courage that doesn't even require kickboxing classes. The courage that defeats fear is not dependent on our own strength—it's dependent on love. And we have *plenty* of love at our fingertips.

First John 4:18 says, *"Perfect love drives out fear."* It is hard to comprehend just how high and how wide and how deep the love of God goes—yet it is completely ours. And because we are loved, we can confess our fear to the God who already knew we were afraid in the first place.

Do you need a healthy dose of courage today? Remember who you are—a child of the King. Call to mind how dearly and completely you are loved by Him. And remember that no matter how hard it tries, fear will never be allowed to live where love already does. There's nothing that can separate you from that love—not circumstances, not weakness, and certainly not fear. When you turn your attention to His perfect love, courage will show up too.

I haven't had many moments when fear has left me alone completely. I still like safety and seatbelts. But fear cannot bully any of us out of doing courageous things because we are way too loved for that.

"Have I not commanded you? Be strong and courageous. Do not be afraid; do not be discouraged, for the LORD your God will be with you wherever you go" (Joshua 1:9).

- What scares you?

- Do you admit your fears, or do you try to hide from them?

- How strongly do you experience God's love, and how does it affect your fear?

Dear Abba, I don't like being afraid, yet I am astounded at how often I feel that way. I want to be braver, stronger, more fearless than I am. In times of fear, help me to remember that it's not strength that stares down fear—it's love. Help me to remember how deeply loved I am by You. Help me to find courage not in my own ability, but in Your fierce and steadfast love. In Your presence and love,

I am strong and courageous.

Amen.

38.

Resolution

*"Take my yoke upon you and learn from me,
for I am gentle and humble in heart..."*
—Matthew 11:29

Do you make New Year's resolutions? I typically don't. To me, a resolution is something I immediately will ignore, avoid, or attempt without hope of much success. Call me an optimist.

If you are like me, you might have a propensity to set unrealistic goals for yourself. Yes, there is a part of us that knows we are overshooting the mark, but that doesn't stop us from demanding perfection. Maybe your resolutions go something like mine ...

—I'm going to lose 25 pounds <u>this</u> month.

—I will keep my office clean no matter what.

—I'm going to read the Bible every day without fail.

—I will keep my legs shaved.

Is it any wonder we avoid resolutions like the plague?

I have a long history of setting myself up for failure. I'm actually quite successful at it. So, imagine what it was like for me to read Matthew 11:28–30: *"Come to me, all you who are weary and burdened, and I will give you rest. Take my yoke upon you and learn from me, for I am gentle and humble in heart, and you will find rest for your souls. For my yoke is easy and my burden is light."* These were some of the first verses of the Bible I ever read. Many years and countless failed resolutions later, I'm still trying to wrap my brain around it. The "weary and burdened" part? Got that. It's the "easy and light" aspect of the verse that often eludes me.

Left to our own devices, we can create incredibly heavy burdens that wrap a yoke around our neck, fitting as comfortably as an itchy wool turtleneck two sizes too small. Worse, we lurch around carrying this heavy weight, barely able to breathe, somehow believing it was God who gave us the burden in the first place. In truth, we have been invited to a life in which God's yoke is easy and His burden is light. Sometimes it's easy to forget this amazing truth in the midst of all the things we want to do and be.

It takes time and conscious awareness to let go of what we believe God demands from us and accept what He actually offers us. When we experience the love and grace of others who demand far less of us than we do of ourselves, as we study God's Word, and as we learn that we're not really capable of anything without the God who is capable of everything, we begin to replace our unreasonable self-demands with the grace and gentleness of the Good Shepherd, who leads us beside still waters.

Jesus is absolutely resolute in His grace for each of us. This year, let us seek to focus on His unwavering, holy resolve instead of hoping for our own. It's the kind of resolution we've needed all along.

- What do you demand of yourself that is unreasonable?

- What are some things you believe God has expected of you that might need to be reexamined in light of His invitation to an easy yoke and a light burden?

- How has God demonstrated His gentleness to you?

My dear Abba, You are so gentle and humble in heart. You want good things for me. Sometimes I lug around so many expectations of myself that I forget

they are not from You. Help me to discern my own harsh expectations from what You truly ask of me. Enlighten me as I read Your Word. Teach me how to embrace and enjoy Your comfort and rest. Help me to trust Your kindness. And as I experience Your unwavering grace, may it transform my own expectations so that I no longer ask more of myself and others than You ever do of me.

In You, I have rest for my soul.

Amen.

39.

Destined for Greatness

*"I can do all this through Him
who gives me strength."*
—Philippians 4:13

Eric Liddell was an Olympic athlete famous for his amazing ability to run like the wind. He was equally famous for his faith in God. When scheduled to run the 100-meter event at the 1924 Olympics on a Sunday, he declined, stating that Sundays were a day of rest from everything—even the sport that he loved. Liddell had a beautiful way of understanding that his faith and his athletic ability were intertwined. In the 1981 movie about his Olympic endeavors, *Chariots of Fire*, he says, *"I believe God made me for a purpose, but He also made me fast. When I run, I feel His pleasure.*"[1] That quote was written for the movie. But his life reflects the same sentiment. Eric Liddell was a living demonstration that we can be salt and light wherever God places us. Some people are just destined for greatness, aren't they?

You are, too, you know.

I'm sure on most days, it doesn't feel like it. Who can aspire to greatness when all we really want is the dishwasher loaded and a pair of jeans that fits well?

For the vast majority of us, greatness doesn't typically happen in big Olympic stadiums for all the world to see. A lot of times, rather, it happens in the smallest decisions that require large amounts of faith.

- Think about that time you chose to forgive the person who wounded you so deeply the scars still remain.

- Then there is that continual decision to stay

quiet when everything in you wants to point out how hard you've worked.

• Remember when you sat with a hurting friend even though you had a to-do list longer than your arm? God does.

He sees it when we choose to respond with kindness instead of anger or when we are brave enough to act even when terrified. Sometimes the greatest moments of our lives are seen only by God. Often, they don't feel great when we are doing them. Forgiveness is hard. Sacrifice is painful. Humility costs. Yet every time we choose those things, a bit more salt and light pours into this world. Hoards of people may never call your name, and you most likely will never receive a gold medal, but you are still destined for greatness.

Eric Liddell's Olympic story was made known throughout the world because *Chariots of Fire* won four Academy Awards, including Best Picture. Even so, Mr. Liddell's true greatness began when his Olympic story ended.

Eric Liddell became a missionary to China a year after his run at the Olympics. Though it was a tumultuous time in that nation's history, Liddell felt compelled to serve there. When Japan invaded China during World War II, Liddell was put into an internment camp with no running water, little food, and bathrooms that were broken. Once again, Eric Liddell demonstrated that we can be salt and light wherever God places us. In the camp, he shared his food when rations were slim, started church services and schools for children, and used humor and grace to ease tensions between prisoners. When he was offered a special release, Liddell gave it to a pregnant woman instead, essentially saving her life and the life of her unborn child.[2]

Liddell acted—one decision, one act of grace, one day at a time that changed the lives of those around him. No one made a movie about that part of his life. He didn't win any medals for it, either. In fact, he died at the age of 43, still interned at the camp, and was buried behind Japanese officers' quarters. His grave, marked by a small wooden cross, was forgotten until it was rediscovered in 1989.

There will be moments in our lives when we are cheered, validated, and celebrated. To be sure, those are times of tremendous joy and blessings. But if you haven't heard the roar of the crowd in a while or added any gold medals to your trophy case lately, your greatest moments are still being witnessed and celebrated by the God who created you and walks with you. When you have placed your life in His hands and trust that His eyes see what others do not, you are indeed destined for greatness.

- Like Eric Liddell as he ran and served, how do you experience God's pleasure in you?

- What do you want your "greatest moments" to be in this life?

Dear Abba, You are a good and gracious God! You have called me to Yourself and destined me to live a life of greatness. It will not always look amazing according to the world's standards. No matter. May I look past desires to be cheered on by the crowd or acknowledged by this world for the things I do. I pray to experience Your pleasure as I live out my calling. And when I stumble and fall, I pray I am lifted once again by the understanding of Your patient, everlasting love. I desire to run this race well. I want to shine Your light wherever I am called to be. May my greatest acts of faith be done for an audience of One—for You alone, my Abba, my Father, my friend, my fortress. With all that I am, with all that You have called me to be, I will praise Your name.

Amen.

40.

Is This It?

When the men came to Jesus, they said, "John the Baptist sent us to you to ask, 'Are you the one who is to come, or should we expect someone else?' "
—Luke 7:20

"Was that it?" Cole's little voice called from his car seat. My mind took a quick inventory of the day: Flying Dumbo ... burgers ... long lines ... Mickey ears ... fireworks ... sunscreen ... funnel cake ... character parade ... Jungle Cruise ... dozens of photographs ... and the Small World theme song stuck like chewed gum in my brain, high-pitched international urchins mercilessly repeating their song like an incantation. Oh, and I was pretty sure we had spent less money on our wedding.

"Yes, Cole, that was it," I sighed. It was midnight, and we were pulling out of the Disneyland parking lot. We had seen it all, done it all, spent it all, and he was somehow disappointed? I closed my eyes, exhausted.

"Was that it?" he asked again. *"Was that Disneyland?"* It took me a minute, and then it dawned on me. Three-year-old Cole wasn't expressing disappointment. Rather, he wanted to know if the place we were driving away from, the place we had explored for the past 15 hours, the place where we'd spun in tea cups and met that giant mouse was the "Disneyland" we'd been telling him about for so long. We had built it up for at least 6 months before we actually went. We told him how much fun it would be and how much he would love it. Cole's mind was attaching the Disneyland he had imagined to what he'd actually experienced. He wanted assurance that he was making the right connection.

Our journey of faith can lead us to have similar questions like my son, Cole. It's a bit disorienting, this life of faith, isn't it? We hear that we can move mountains with just a bit of faith, but most days we can't even keep up with the laundry. *Is this it?* we wonder, mostly to ourselves because we're not sure where else to go with the question. The question is far too big yet far too personal for this world to answer satisfactorily.

Maybe we're afraid to ask God *"Is this it?"* for fear of sounding ungrateful or disappointed. Maybe we think we shouldn't be asking a lot of questions because we should just trust. Maybe we are afraid God won't answer. Maybe we are afraid He will.

Scripture gives us a strong picture of who God is and who He isn't. As the source of truth, the Word of God is the best place to explore the nature of His character and the way He feels about His people. It's also a great place to discover that God's people ask questions, a lot of them. Some of the questions are fueled by doubt. Some by faith. Some by wonder. Some are the result of extreme pain and others of incredible joy. The point is that God's people are asking ... and asking.

God is unafraid of our questions, so we don't need to be either. Allow the deepest questions of your heart to form. Write them down on paper if that helps. Then take them to the only One who can answer the essence of what we really need to know.

In Scripture, John the Baptist was a man with a vision. He prepared the way of the Lord. He preached and prophesied with confidence that the Messiah was coming. When Jesus began His public ministry, it was John who recognized Him, baptized Him, and testified that Jesus was the Chosen One.

But somewhere along the line, what John imagined about the coming of the Messiah and what he actually experienced diverged. Early on in Jesus' ministry, John was carried off to prison, certain death looming. It was in the cold darkness of his cell that John sent word to Jesus: *"Is this it?"*

John needed to know if the unexpected and disheartening events that had unfolded were supposed to be happening, or if he made a mistake about Jesus. Maybe there was someone else or something else that was to come.

When life throws us curveballs and we are imprisoned by depression, grief, or circumstances beyond our control, our feelings might be similar to John's. We long to know if this is it, or if we should be expecting something else. If John went to Jesus with his doubt, his fear, his confusion, then it seems a good bet we can too.

And how did Jesus respond?

He said, *"Go back and report to John what you have seen and heard: The blind receive sight, the lame walk, those who have leprosy are cleansed, the deaf* hear, the dead are raised, and the good news is proclaimed to the poor" (Luke 7:22).

In other words, Jesus invited John to remember what he had already seen, heard, and experienced for himself. He asked John to connect what he knew of God's Word to the life that was in front of him. John needed to attach the Messiah he imagined to what he experienced. Jesus' response assured John he was making the right connection—even if the particulars were not exactly what he had pictured.

When this journey of faith doesn't align with what we imagined, we might feel less sure, less steady on our feet. We can regain our footing by walking in the footsteps of the faithful who came before us, by asking questions and looking to Jesus for the answers. Sometimes we just need to be reminded of all we have seen and heard.

Yes, this is it. In all its fragility and beauty, doubt and joy, pain and peace, this is the life we have been invited to. It will never quite be what we've expected, but it will always be a place where God will do (and has done) more marvelous things than we can even imagine. The blind will see, the lame will walk, and the things we thought most dead in our lives can rise again.

And that is very, very good news.

- How have your expectations of God differed from your experience of Him?

- When you are worried, afraid, or doubting, do you turn to God with your questions, or do you keep them to yourself? Why?

- What have you seen God do in your life?

Dear Abba, teach me to attach the truth of who You are to what I imagine about You. Let Your Word

guide my path. Help me to remember that when I am confused, afraid, or disillusioned, You want me to come to You with all of my questions. This life is beautiful and complicated, and I need Your truth to guide my path. I pray to discover more of You, Your goodness, Your faithfulness, Your grace. Allow me to see where I am blind. Find the elements of my life that have been dead for far too long and bring them to life again. May I bear witness to Your miraculous, unexpected, marvelous ways.

I praise You for all You are.

Amen.

Acknowledgments

When I reflect on the people who have been with me on this journey, my heart floods with gratitude. I am humbled and amazed that God has somehow seen fit to bring people into my life who continue to point me back to Him—to His goodness, His faithfulness, His generosity.

To my editor and friend, Tricia Bennett—Not only did you agree to take on this project, you embraced it, and in doing so, you embraced me. Your enthusiasm, dedication, intuition, feedback, and gentle, guiding questions were a compelling force and undergirding support throughout this process. I am forever grateful.

To my Sunday night dinner group—Thanks for reminding me that I need to have a regular appointment with fun, food, and friends that feel like family. Without you, I fear I would be shuffling around the house in my pajamas, unshowered and mumbling about how much work there is to be done. I love that we get to live this life together.

To Nancy Stemme—Your tenacity is what brought me to my first Bible study, and all these years later, it's still your faithfulness in God and to our friendship that has given me the gift of being known.

To Duane Grobman—Your gentleness and wisdom have taught me about the importance of rest—in God, His plan, and His pleasure in me. You are an abiding source of solace, respite, and fantastic book recommendations. I'm grateful for all three.

To Steve Marckley—When I was in need, you were there. You have been generous with your counsel, friendship, and belief that it was all going to be okay. And it was, wasn't it?

To Mom and Dad—When you moved nearby, you thought it was because you would need my help in the near future. As it turns out, I needed yours. The countless last-minute favors, endless trips picking up and dropping off Elizabeth, the delicious dinners, folded laundry, and washed dishes have been a lifeline. Thank you for making my crazy life manageable and being excited for all my adventures. I love you both so very much.

To Mark Gould—You saw my artistic heart when I didn't. You've given me the gift of your directing talents, creative eye, and unwavering friendship. I am not only a better communicator because of you, I am a better person. Let's keep dreaming up new stuff, okay?

To the women of NorthPark Community Church, both past and present—You gave me the privilege of serving you for 12 years. When I felt led to pursue writing and speaking, you gave me your enthusiastic blessing and support. Through you, I learned about encouragement, kindness, hard work, faith, and the value of a great afternoon tea. It was an honor of a lifetime to serve as your Director of Women's Ministry. You have a permanent place in my heart.

To Nicole Johnson—You saw what I could not. Thanks for holding this new chapter safely in your hands until I was ready to turn the page. You have been a mentor, friend, and inspiration, and I am forever grateful.

To the Seasons Weekend team—This is all your fault, you know. Without your care, artistry, transparency, wisdom, and humor, I wouldn't have known that my deepest longings were guideposts to a richer, deeper, truer life in Jesus Christ. I've been changed by your love, your talents, your vulnerabilities, and your stories in the best possible way. Thank you, my friends.

To my family—Danny, Elizabeth, and Cole—You are my home, my heart, and the loves of my life. Thank you for your support, your encouragement, and your patience while I figured out how to pursue my dreams and still (sometimes) make dinner. Without you, I would be lost. I love this life we've carved out for ourselves and can't wait to see what adventure we will go on next. As long as I'm with you, I'll go anywhere.

Finally, to my Savior, Redeemer, Solace, and Rest, Jesus Christ—Thanks for finding me, scooping me up, and inviting me into Your grace. I pray my life is, in some small measure, a reflection of Your freedom and joy. To You alone I give my praise, worship, and adoration, forever and always, with all that I am.

NOTES

Chapter 3
1. Van Gogh, Vincent. "To Theo vanGogh." 9 Sep. 1882. Original Manuscript. Amsterdam, Van Gogh Museum, inv. nos.b251 a-b V/1962.

Chapter 5
1. Buechner, Frederick. *Beyond Words: Daily Readings in the ABC's of Faith.* Harper San Francisco, 2004.

Chapter 6
1. Hustead, Ted. "History of Wall Drug." *Wall Drug Store,* www.walldrug.com/history/since-1931. Accessed 10 Nov. 2015.

Chapter 8
1. Nouwen, Henri J.M. *A Cry for Mercy: Prayers from the Genesee.* Doubleday, 1981.

Chapter 13
1. Gilbert, Elizabeth. "Your Elusive Creative Genius." TED. Feb. 2009. Lecture.

Chapter 18
1. To learn more about Jay & Katherine Wolf and their ministry, visit www.HopeHeals.com.

Chapter 22
1. Lewis, C.S. *The Lion, the Witch, and the Wardrobe.* Geoffrey Bles, 1950.

Chapter 30
1. Manning, Brennan. *A Glimpse of Jesus: the Stranger to Self-Hatred.* Harper San Francisco, 2004.

Chapter 31
1. *The Shawshank Redemption.* Directed by Frank Darabont, Castle Rock Entertainment, 1994.
2. For information and help for those affected by suicide, as well as depression and anxiety, please visit www.hope4mentalhealth.com.

Chapter 34
1. Van Biema, David. "Her Agony." *Time Magazine* 10 Sep. 2007, page 40.
2. Manning, Brennan. *Abba's Child: The Cry of the Heart for Intimate Belonging.* NavPress, 2002.

Chapter 39
1. *Chariots of Fire.* Directed by Hugh Hudson, Warner Bros. Studios, 1981.
2. Smallwood, Karl. "The Heroic Death of Chariots of Fire's Eric Liddell." *Today I Found Out,* 12 Dec. 2013, http://www.todayifoundout.com/index.php/2013/12/heroic-death-chariots-fires-eric-liddell/.